Endorsements

For decades, I have both learned from and respected Gordon's biblical knowledge and teaching. I am blessed to know him not only as an outstanding Bible teacher, but also as a dear friend. But perhaps the quality I most admire in Gordon is his humility. It requires humility to rethink and restudy long-held presuppositions, but his love for the Word and his desire to please God continually call him back to this posture.

Years ago, in response to his studies on the biblical call for justice, Gordon began addressing racial injustices he saw filtering from the world into the church. While some may have questioned his focus at that time, it would soon become a major issue for discussion and change in the churches. His teaching helped set the stage for many in the church to dive deeper into their understandings of God's calls to justice. Because Gordon so deeply respects the Scriptures and the leading of the Spirit, he is not afraid to be a prophetic voice addressing needed change. For me, as one who has often struggled with pleasing people, this is such an admirable, necessary quality for a church striving to join God in His purposes.

When I began studying the role of women in the church about eight years ago, I was challenged by many things I was learning. When I asked Gordon for input on my book about the subject, he disagreed with my thoughts and reacted negatively. Yet, in response to my questions, he began a deep study and changed many of his pre-held understandings of scriptures applicable to this subject, which he shares in the following pages. His courage, combined with humility keeps him growing and changing, and allows us the opportunity to grow along with him.

While many books have been written on this topic, Gordon offers some new perspectives for us to ponder. He has written, not to create conflict, but to help us rethink and reapply some of our understanding of scriptures that prayerfully bring us closer to God's divine will for which we were created. He calls those who may come to different conclusions to appropriately view these issues as disputable matters, allowing us to practice unity in diversity. Thank you, Gordon, for continuing to learn and teach with humility and careful study of Scripture. And, thank you for your courage and prophetic edge that calls us all to think and grow. Though through illness he nearly finished his life on earth in 2022, I thank God he blessed us by giving him more years and put this important teaching on his heart.

Jeanie Shaw
DMin, Spiritual Formation and Discipleship
Teacher, Author, Christian life coach

There are times when a subject or issue seems straightforward and easy to understand, but when we take a closer look, we may find nuances and a depth that we didn't catch. There are even times when we miss the basic point altogether, while we major in what are really minors. In this book, my friend Gordon Ferguson is calling us to do what we need to do with many biblical subjects, and that is to take another look and go deeper to consider some things we may have missed.

In the Genesis account, we read that "God created mankind in his own image, in the image of God he created them; male and female he created them." In these words, Gordon finds the main point regarding the relationship of males and females. Jesus no doubt shocked his culture and world by practicing the truth of this message. The equality taught here may have received lip service through the centuries, but in reality, there has been something far different practiced. The norm has been a heavy-handed, possessive, and defensive patriarchy. Even a gentler version of this idea still does not reflect even dimly the deep truth found in this text and elaborated on in other texts.

Disturbed by the injustice that this has created and the damage it has done to women, Gordon takes us on a deep dive into a subject that he has been revisiting for more than five years. However, to benefit in any way from his research and study, we must start by recognizing how deeply ingrained a different view is in most of our hearts and minds, particularly in those of us who are male, but often in female minds as well. And then we must humbly ask God to help us approach this subject with a radical openness. Ironically, some of us who have studied the Bible the longest will have the most difficulty setting aside a certain paradigm through which we have looked at scripture in order to see what God really intended. That is, no doubt, true of many subjects, but there is something about this matter and the emotions it creates that makes it even more challenging.

This prayer that we find at the end of Psalm 139 is an amazing model for us in many arenas.

Search me, God, and know my heart;
test me and know my anxious thoughts.
See if there is any offensive way in me,
and lead me in the way everlasting.

It is my belief that all who come to this work in the spirit of this prayer, will go away with a deep appreciation for the work that Gordon has done and fresh understanding that will help us, males and females, to be the people of God, more like Jesus our Lord, going forward in these modern times. I would never say if you are humble that you will agree with all his conclusions. However, I commend Gordon's thinking to you and trust you will give it open-minded consideration, especially in view of his long career of seeking the deeper things in Scripture, and making changes in his own thinking and life.

Tom A. Jones
Teacher, Author
Founding Editor, Discipleship Publications International

Two concerning recent cultural trends in society threaten to overtake American church culture as well. The first is cancel culture. A 2023 survey indicated that 64% of Americans are very familiar with the concept of cancel culture. This is up from 44% percent in 2020. If someone doesn't think like us or express ideas that we find acceptable, then cancel culture dictates that they be silenced, shamed, and have their public influence canceled. Cancel culture threatens new ideas, rigorous debate, and mutual respect. In the Christian version, practices that we don't like or biblical views with which we disagree are labeled as sinful or unbiblical and we seek to prevent them from making their case or influencing others.

The second problematic trend is what can be called purity spiral testing. This has grown exponentially in the American political culture. While it has always been a potential problem for followers of Jesus, the proliferation of it in the world of politics has started to creep back into church culture more and more. The purity spiral test demands that others agree with us on every point, or they will be labeled and marginalized as not really being one of us.

There is little question that what Gordon has written here will challenge many readers. Some will read this and see it as a welcome change. Others will read it with suspicion and concern. The easy road to cancel culture and purity spiral testing is to simply label things we don't like or agree with as unbiblical, claiming that the authority of Scripture is at stake. That is a uniquely Christian method of shutting down healthy debate and conversation. It also ignores the spirit of Paul's words in Romans 14:1–15:7 by casting virtually any issue as a de facto salvation issue, which means that discussing this topic is now dangerous.

Remaining rooted in Paul's exhortation to the Romans is vital when it comes to ongoing discussions revolving around the role of women in the church community. There are without question differing views on this topic, the spectrum that ranges from strict complementarian to ardent egalitarian, as an example. Adding to the confusion, in my opinion, is that Paul appears to have been more of a pragmatist for the sake of the gospel than neatly falling into any of today's ideological camps.

He was willing to prescribe limitations in specific situations where the cultural context demanded it (such as in Corinth) but also seemed to embrace no restrictions in situations like Rome or Laodicea where such boundaries might themselves serve as an obstacle to the message of the gospel. Paul was willing to be all things to all people for the sake of the gospel. But because he seems to utilize varying strategies in different situations, it is easy for different camps on the women's role issue to find language that supports their view and allows them to dismiss the other view as an error.

Gordon has pulled off the difficult task of exploring a difficult and controversial topic with grace, clarity, and simplicity. He brings some much-needed fresh perspective to a topic that has been covered by many scholars but very few have done so from the practical and pastoral angle that this book provides. I highly recommend this book and think that even those who don't find themselves agreeing with everything Gordon says, will still be provoked and challenged to think in new ways. No one will regret reading *Women in the Bible: How Did I Miss So Much?*

Michael Burns

DMin, Biblical and Theological Engagement

International Teacher and Author

Women in the Bible
How Did I Miss So Much?

NOTE: Throughout the book, Bible quotations will be from the New American Standard Bible (NASB) or the New International Version (NIV) unless otherwise noted. The NIV edition is the 2011 edition. The NASB edition used will be the 1995 edition, although a 2020 version is now available. The earlier editions (1971 and 1977), along with the 1995 edition, have carried the most influence in the historical setting I am addressing. In our present setting, I will be quoting from the NIV without noting it but will note when I am quoting from the NASB.

About the author: Gordon Ferguson is a graduate of Northwestern State University and the Harding School of Theology. With more than fifty years of experience, he has served as an evangelist, elder and teacher. Gordon has written eighteen books and produced many audio/video teaching series. He and his wife, Theresa,  make their home in McKinney, Texas. For additional information about his work and ministry go to www.GordonFerguson.org.

Theatron Press is an imprint of Illumination Publishers International

Contents

Acknowledgments

Having written numerous books, I have accordingly written many acknowledgments. I am indebted to more people than I could possibly name for helping me discover my spiritual gifts, develop them, and then use them for well over half a century in ministry. Writing is one of those gifts, and as Eric Liddell said of his gift in the movie *Chariots of Fire,* when I am using those gifts I feel God's pleasure. For all those men and women in my past who were used by God to influence and mold me, I am beyond grateful. My wife of 59 years, Theresa, has been a source of unlimited patience, encouragement, and love. Details of our amazing relationship can be readily seen in my book, *Fairy Tales Do Come True!*[1] I also offer a special shout-out to my spiritually adopted daughter, Kelly Flores, who read my manuscript and gave me input from her perspective gained from the corporate and educational fields. But here, I want to focus almost exclusively on the three who wrote endorsements for my book.

As is mentioned in several of the ensuing chapters, Jeanie Shaw somehow took an older man with a heightened sense of resistance to broadening his perspective of women's roles in the church and then watched me as my resistance turned into a passion. She was an amazingly effective tool in God's hands in the process, and I am most grateful to her and God. You will gain further insight into our relationship as you read about her influence on me as both a dear friend and mentor. She and her now departed husband, Wyndham, have blessed my life, ministry, and marriage in delightfully positive ways. As a result, their names can be found in not a few of my books.

Tom Jones and I met for the first time in 1983 when we were both speakers at a conference in Southern California, and by God's providence were assigned to the same hotel room. I was having

---

1. Gordon Ferguson, *Fairy Tales Do Come True: 16 Principles to Ensure That You Live Happily Every After* (Spring, TX: Illumination Publishers, 2016).

something like a midlife spiritual crisis at the time and carried on a conversation into the wee hours of the night with him, loaded with question after question. He demonstrated great patience with me then and has continued to do so in the years since, for we were destined from the start to become the closest of spiritual brothers. When I had tabled the publication of this book, Tom was the catalyst for helping me reconsider, and then he and Jeanie worked together to help me finish the process.

Michael Burns became a friend and mentor from a distance when I first started writing and speaking about racial issues. He granted me the privilege of reading the manuscripts of his three books on racial and ethnic topics, the best three of their type I have ever read. Now Michael is a teaching minister at the same church in Dallas-Fort Worth of which I am a member, which has allowed us to deepen our friendship in person. Michael is a popular speaker at churches both nationally and internationally and is a regular teaching contributor in the Ministry Training Academies in Johannesburg, Nairobi, Lagos, and Abidjan. His contributions to my thinking about women in the Bible have been significant and much appreciated.

Including myself along with these three, we have authored cumulatively over seventy books, on a very wide variety of biblically related topics. The total number of books we have read would likely be a rather staggering number, one known but to God. These broad experiences give me confidence, not simply in our collective collaboration, but in God using it all to make this book you are about to read a worthwhile addition to the ongoing discussion of a topic of great importance.

An *Essential* Introduction

Sometimes we skip introductions, especially if they don't catch our eye quickly. I pray that the word "essential" caught your attention, and you are reading this rather than already reading Chapter 1. The topic of this book is controversial and has been for a long, long time. It is even more controversial now than ever before, based on recent events in American Christianity, as will be addressed in Chapter 1.

Although I firmly believe it should fall into the realm of opinion matters, much like the subjects discussed in Romans 14, many people will not allow that. They may freely admit that it doesn't fall within the realm of salvation matters and is not nearly as important as topics like the Deity of Christ, his incarnation, crucifixion, and literal resurrection from the dead, yet they feel compelled to find or invent a category that makes it important enough to disallow its inclusion in the realm of opinion matters. Whether they realize it or not, at that point it has become a salvation matter in that they believe it can incite God's strong disapproval if viewed and applied wrongly. I find this very sad.

Variations in Practice Should Exist

When the New Covenant was inaugurated as described in Acts 2, Peter tied in those current events with prophecies from Joel 2. The outpouring of the Holy Spirit was to introduce sons and daughters prophesying and male and female servants of God prophesying (Acts 2:17–18). While that must have been quite surprising, given the male dominated leadership of Israel, it is stated plainly enough so that its practice should have been expected as an integral part of God's family going forward.

While that should have been the expectation, the specifics of how it would look in practice were yet to be worked out. As it was worked out, the existing culture of any given location affected its practice. The church in Corinth had women prophesying, but there were necessary cultural considerations which rightly affected the practice. The church in Ephesus had a different cultural issue, for what was said in the letter to the Corinthian church was not found in the letter to the Ephesians, and vice versa.

That is important, by the way, for repetitions or near repetitions are not uncommon in Paul's epistles. For example, consider the many parallels in Colossians and Ephesians and between elder qualities in 1 Timothy 3 and Titus 1. Thus, it is necessary to figure out, as best we can 2000 years later, what those cultural considerations were surrounding the role of women and whether they are the same as those we have today in any location. Furthermore, we must also consider whether or not they contain principles that should have a different application today.

Suffice it to say that what might not raise eyebrows in a California church will raise more than eyebrows in Africa or the Middle East. That must be considered carefully. Cultural considerations are real and important. Although Western countries like the United States are far more progressive in what women do in many aspects of our society, even the US has a fairly wide range of cultural differences regarding male and female church participation. What might be considered quite acceptable culturally in Oregon might not be considered quite as acceptable in another state with historically deeper roots in male chauvinism (like my home state of Louisiana).

Another Source Producing Variations

Besides cultural considerations in society and in the church, variations in practice will occur because of local church leadership and their own judgment and choices. We have variations between churches in a number of areas. I could list some of those areas of differences as could you, but we seem to be comfortable with many of our variations in how we do church. Yet when discussing how women participate in the church, especially in church services, and most especially in Sunday services, we may quickly lose that comfortability. In many other areas we say that it is really not our business how another leadership decides to do church where they are, but we may well not have that same tolerance and acceptance when it comes to the women's role.

Romans 14 is in the New Testament for a reason. The matters discussed there, primarily the eating of meats and observance of days, were huge issues in the early church. They were nothing like some of our easily tolerated differences to which we just alluded. They were not merely matters of preference. In the setting of Jewish Christians and Gentile Christians learning to live together as a united family in spite of their different backgrounds and different understandings, these were issues that could have done great spiritual harm. How did God handle it? Not by a legal approach of spelling out just what should and should not be done in all cases, but by teaching tolerance and acceptance of differences. We would do well to stop right here and read Romans 14 slowly and carefully now. In fact, please do.

My Challenges as a Writer

Writing on this topic is fraught with challenges. Because of the availability of modern means of instant communication, people in different cultures in various parts of the world will be reading this. I have to trust that in reading my introduction, they will give due consideration to their own culture and not make knee-jerk changes that will hurt their spiritual family. I beg you to do that rather than allow yourself to have an emotional reaction to what you are about to read in the remainder of this book.

I also understand that what I write might not be as understandable to you as I would hope it is. Almost all who study communication say that words alone comprise no more than 10% of the communication process. That is both staggering and scary to contemplate. You cannot see my facial expressions or other body language. You cannot hear my voice with its volume, variations of volume, inflection, and speech rate. You may assume accurately what those might be like as you read my words, but you might just as easily assume inaccurately. For this reason, please feel free to write or call to ask questions. This will allow other parts of the communication process to fill in some blanks or clarify what is unclear just from reading my words.

I am writing as one person, hence giving one man's opinion. There are those who believe that no controversial topic should be addressed by an individual, but rather must be addressed by a committee or group of qualified people. I could raise questions about who in a group is really qualified, what makes them qualified, and who decides that, but this is not my point here. I will observe that the Catholic Church, the Mormon Church, the Jehovah's Witnesses, and a number of other religious organizations have all but perfected communal theology and the unity it produces within their particular group. That example alone should make the point that truth trumps unity, as important as unity is. The Pharisees and Sadducees of Jesus' day were united within their own groups, but that unity did not attract praise from Jesus. Quite the contrary.

Had my books on church leadership been produced by groups, they would have read quite differently, trust that. But there must always be a place for a prophetic voice to raise questions and voice concerns that others do not. By prophetic, I do not mean directly inspired by the Holy Spirit like the Bible was, but rather a dissonant voice asking for a reexamination of views that might just be based on tradition rather than truth. To that end, I write this material and ask only that you consider it carefully along with all else that you study on the topic. Never assume that you have exhausted any topic, especially complex ones, and that you now have all the answers. You don't, nor do I. My view of a teacher's role is that we should carefully study complex topics and then present them in a way that neither compromises truth nor confuses the average listener or reader.

But Why Now, Gordon?

That is a very relevant question, one that I have asked myself scores of time as I have written this material. I have entertained many second thoughts about writing and publishing this book from its inception. The question in the back of my mind was, "Should I, or shouldn't I?" The root cause prompting that question centered around a one-word question, "Why?"

My own reservations from the start came from a sense that my family of churches, like most other denominations, were already reeling from changes in the world and thus in the church that were all but impossible to negotiate. The rapidity of changes in the world, in our country, in our region of the country, and in the church is overwhelming. Combine these overwhelming changes with a worldwide pandemic and the reentry into the "Cold War" with its real threats of escalation, most of us find ourselves just trying to hang on for dear life. The world has gone mad. We long for a return to some semblance of the more ordinary life we have experienced up to the past decade or so.

With all of this forced upon us, why deal with a topic that might add to the tensions among those in our group? It is a valid question I have considered in conversations with others. Surely, unity is a huge issue in our heavenly Father's heart. Jesus' prayer for complete unity in John 17 has always been staggering to contemplate, now more than ever in our world, fueled by social media judgments, condemnations, shaming, and cancelling. But as I will mention later in the book, biblical truth trumps unity, especially fundamental truths.

What are fundamental biblical truths? In the midst of condemning a whole litany of practices by the Pharisees, Jesus said this: "Woe to you, teachers of the law and Pharisees, you hypocrites! You give a tenth of your spices—mint, dill, and cumin. But you have neglected the more important matters of the law—justice, mercy, and faithfulness. You should have practiced the latter, without neglecting the former" (Matthew 23:23). In exalting the importance of justice, mercy, and faithfulness, he was reflecting these words of the prophet in Micah 6:8 (NASB). "He has told you, O man, what is good; And what does the LORD require of you but to do justice, to love kindness, and to walk humbly with your God?"

Justice is a driving force in my heart. I have been addressing racial issues for nearly a decade in speech and in writing, compelled by seeing injustice in this realm permeate our society, often subtly and unrecognized by those perpetrating it. For me, righteous indignation is the only possible reaction. Sexism, more often called misogyny in our current setting, has so much in common with systemic racism. Few White folks or male folks in America can keep their terminology from exposing its roots in these systemic ills which clearly fall under the banner of injustice. That said, I offer no apologies for speaking out against injustice in any form, certainly not in these two areas that affect our churches.

Another reason I wrote is that this discussion is not going away. Jeanie Shaw's book, *The View from Paul's Window*,[2] let the horse out of the barn, as her late and great husband used to say. An official team of teachers in our movement added their own book, prompted in part by the teaching of others that was at the time outside the box of our traditional beliefs and practices. The horse is so far out of the barn that the barn is now nowhere to be seen. There is no turning back. The discussions will continue, and both individual Christians and churches will make their decisions of interpretation and subsequent practices based upon those interpretations.

So, to summarize and be clear, my goal in writing this book is to promote justice for women, my sisters in Christ, who seek to use their gifts from God to serve him, and to do it at a time when many are wrestling with these issues and when a new generation is considering their relationship to the Christian community and to the Bible. If I accomplish my goal, it will not only mean better

---

2. Jeanie Shaw, *The View from Paul's Window: Paul's Teachings on Women* (Spring, TX: Illumination Publishers, 2020).

things for women who seek to follow Jesus, but it will mean much better things for men as well, and that means for the whole Body of Christ.

I won't have the last word to say on the topic, nor would I want to. It is an ongoing discussion, and I obviously believe an important one. To those who think that my book could lead to further division, I say that it could just as well lead to further unity. I don't believe what I have written is necessarily unique, but I believe the way I say it contains enough uniqueness to warrant its publication. As is oft repeated, hordes of our young people are leaving the church. One of the reasons, although certainly not the only one by any means, is in our failure to keep up with the times as much as the Bible allows (and calls us to). How we view women in the church is a significant part of that failure.

Please keep studying this issue. It is far more important than most of our older members now realize. Let what I have written help awaken you to that fact, and let it add one more source to your study efforts. Until I die, which at my age cannot be too far away, I will speak against injustices, and for reasons known but to God he chose an old man born into the depths of racism and male chauvinism to speak out on these two types of systemic injustice. I cannot do otherwise, so help me God! Whether you end up agreeing with me or not, just give my observations careful consideration. I ask no more than that. Thank you in advance for following this recommendation.

Chapter 1

A Historical Perspective

The more I study women in the Bible and how their examples should affect our view of women in our churches, the more amazed I am at how much I (we) have missed. When I say missed, I'm not just talking about missing rather obvious insights, but about so much regarding who God designed women to be and to do in our families and in our churches. I personally am embarrassed and ashamed of my own failures to see some things that were clear, and I must begin by apologizing to women in general and certainly to those female friends of mine in the church, including my own wife of 59 years. And I must thank them for their patience with me and for helping the scales start falling off my spiritual eyes.

But what of the question posed in the title? How did I miss so much? I think the answer boils down to a few essential items. One, I (we) have often misunderstood/misinterpreted two passages in the beginning of the Bible—one in Genesis 2 and one in Genesis 3. Two, we have misunderstood/misinterpreted three passages in Paul's epistles. In all five cases, our interpretations have often failed to consider their contexts, especially cultural contexts. Three, we have made one broad, yet I believe incorrect assumption, based on these interpretations which has led to further incorrect assumptions contained in both the Old Testament and New Testament.

This may sound like a lot to unpack, and in some ways, it is. But when we start dealing with the five specific passages, I believe you will feel like you are watching a puzzle fall into place. However, before we start this biblical unpacking, some introductory material is needed to provide an important backstory to help us see the bigger picture historically.

Signs of the Times

Whether we recognize it or not, our churches are at several crossroads moments right now, with others, no doubt, soon to follow. One of these is the place of women in our church life. The radical differences of how women are viewed and function in society to how they are viewed and function in the church put us at a crossroads. Do these differences in society and in the church matter? Should they matter? Christianity by its very design is countercultural. But it should only be countercultural when the Bible demands it, not by holding on to our traditions.

To influence the most people possible, we need to adjust to everything in current culture that we can without violating God's stated will. A quick read of Paul's comments in 1 Corinthians 9 makes that point difficult to miss.

1 Corinthians 9:19–23

[19] Though I am free and belong to no one, I have made myself a slave to everyone, to win as many as possible. [20] To the Jews I became like a Jew, to win the Jews. To those under the law I became like one under the law (though I myself am not under the law), so as to win those under the law. [21] To those not having the law I became like one not having the law (though I am not free from God's law but am under Christ's law), so as to win those not having the law. [22] To the weak I became weak, to win the weak. I have become all things to all people so that by all possible means I might save some. [23] I do all this for the sake of the gospel, that I may share in its blessings.

I have heard it said (repeatedly) that if we allow culture to influence how women function in the church, then other cultural issues will follow. That is to me one amazing assumption and will not be true if we follow the Bible. It is like comparing apples to grapefruits. Regarding women's functions in the church, we are talking about women doing what they did in the Bible with God's approval, in both the Old Testament and New Testament. Regarding immoral aspects of our culture, I am referring to areas specifically in violation of the Bible. If the Scriptures approve one thing and condemn another, how can they both be forced to fit into the same package? The fact that some will inevitably try to fit them together is not a valid reason for failing to separate them and to deal with each biblically.

That doesn't mean that biblically illiterate people won't try to lump everything together. Of course they will. They don't accept the Bible as the basis for their beliefs and practices. But Bible believing people should not, decidedly not.

This is Not Just a Recent Discussion

Some people in our family of churches may be scratching their heads wondering why we seem to be suddenly discussing women's roles in the church and even becoming embroiled in debate-type discussions. Why this topic and why this topic now? How did we get here in the first place? We are not new to these discussions, and they are finally making their way into our fellowship of churches. These discussions have been taking place in the Evangelical world all around us for well over thirty years.

Plus, they have been taking place in our parent churches, the Mainstream Churches of Christ, for many more decades. Furthermore, in the early 1990s, we had our own discussions and as a result, significantly broadened the role of women in our family of churches. Prior to that time, women did not serve as ushers, pass the communion and collection trays, baptize other women, or share in any way in front of the church—part-singing included. If you were around then, you may recall some of the lessons that teachers like Douglas Jacoby and I taught that helped us shed some of our traditions in this regard. Let's delve into at least a brief view of some of this history as a precursor to digging into the Bible itself.

Discussions in the Evangelical World

The battle lines that were drawn distinctively by the 1990s were between what came to be called the Egalitarians and the Complementarians. The former group, often called biblical feminists, are the more progressive. They believe that a woman's spiritual giftset should determine her roles and functions in the church rather than simply her gender. The latter group, often called hierarchicalists or complementarians, believe that women are limited by God's intentions in much the same way that they have been limited throughout most of human history—always subject to the leadership of men and occupying much lesser roles. Thus, the man is the head or leader of women, and women are by divine design to be submissive to the leadership of man in the home and church (and possibly in all settings, some would say). This view emphasizes that these limitations should not be used to justify men disrespecting or abusing women, but it must be maintained when it comes to roles and functions in both home and church.

New parachurch organizations were formed to support each position: The Council on Biblical Manhood and Womanhood (CBMW, 1987) representing complementarians and Christians for Biblical Equality (CBE International, 1988), representing egalitarians. Wayne Grudem is listed as the founder of CBMW, and he, along with John Piper, edited what I call their "Bible," with the title of *Recovering Biblical Manhood and Womanhood.* The subtitle is "A Response to Evangelical Feminism."[3]

According to my research, the egalitarian group formed in a meeting at the home of Catherine and Richard Kroeger in Massachusetts. The basic tenets of their foundational beliefs are briefly contained in a document entitled, "Men, Women, and Biblical Equality." This two-page document can be downloaded as a PDF file in a number of different languages on the CBE International

---

3. Wayne Grudem and John Piper, *Recovering Biblical Manhood and Womanhood: A Response to Evangelical Feminism* (Wheaton, IL: Crossway, 2021), Kindle.

website.[4] This was followed by what I now call their "Bible," also written by a consortium of authors, *Discovering Biblical Equality*, edited by Ronald Pierce and Rebecca Groothuis, with Gordon Fee listed as the Contributing Editor. This book's subtitle is "*Complementarity Without Hierarchy*."[5]

The discussions and disagreements between the two groups have resulted in the writing of many books and hundreds of articles over the last several decades. Sides have been drawn and consequences have varied, ranging from calm to heated discussions with actions taken. Ministry positions and theological teaching positions have become a testing ground for how seriously these views have affected the evangelical world, with firings and hirings resulting from the views one holds. The battle is picking up steam even as I write this chapter.

A Very Current Example

In February 2023, the Southern Baptist Convention (SBC), which is the largest Protestant denomination in the US, voted to expel five churches for appointing women pastors to key positions. One of these churches is quite well-known, led for years by Rick Warren, a popular preacher and author. The Saddleback Church is (was) the second largest in the SBC, so this move was quite surprising, even shocking. In an article in the January 15, 2023, online issue of *The Week*, Peter Weber writes:

> When Saddleback's founding pastor, Rick Warren, retired last August, he put a married couple, pastors Andy and Stacie Wood, in charge of the megachurch. With more than 23,000 members and 12 locations in Southern California, "Saddleback is a household name in American evangelical Christianity," *The Nashville Tennessean* reports.... "Southern Baptists hold to a complementarianism, a theological idea

---

4. cbmw.org
5. Ronald W. Pierce, Rebecca Merrill Groothuis, Gordon D. Fee, *Discovering Biblical Equality: Complementarity Without Hierarchy* (Westmont, IL: IVP Academic, 2005).

that teaches men and women have certain assigned roles." Saddleback and the other four churches expelled Tuesday were judged to be in violation of the SBC's stated belief that "while both men and women are gifted for service in the church, the office of pastor is limited to men as qualified by Scripture." Saddleback has been under scrutiny at the Southern Baptist Convention since it ordained three women as pastors in May 2021, and some Southern Baptists tried to get the church expelled at national meeting in 2021 and 2022.[6]

Update on Rick Warren and the SBC

The Southern Baptist Convention, at their New Orleans convention on June 14, 2023, voted to uphold a previous ruling reached in February to expel the Saddleback church and four others from the SBC. Three of the churches appealed the earlier ruling and lost their appeal. Of the 11,000-plus messengers present during the time of the vote, 9,437 messengers (88.46%) voted to uphold the removal of Saddleback Church, with 1,212 (11.36%) voting to allow the church to remain part of the Convention. Warren said that he was not surprised, although he had given a previous speech encouraging the upcoming vote to turn in their favor.

Rick made one statement that would likely be true of almost any long-established religious organization. "The face of Southern Baptists does not look at all like our annual meeting."[7] Most such organizations, including those among my particular fellowship, the ICOC (International Churches of Christ), remain governed by older males, many of whom have allowed a chasm to develop between themselves and the majority of their membership, especially the younger generations. In my words, as I strive to reflect the words of Jesus, many who were once new wine breaking old wineskins have become old wineskins themselves and don't realize it. I

---

6. Peter Weber, "Southern Baptists expel Saddleback," *The Week*, January 15, 2023.
7. "Southwest Seminary Preview Day," *Baptist Standard: Connecting God's Story and God's People*, April 12, 2023, https://www.baptiststandard.com/news/baptists/sbc-affirms-ouster-of-churches-with-female-pastors/ .

have engaged in much study and many conversations that caused me to adjust my wineskins. I believe that whenever the leadership becomes the old wineskins and remains out of touch with the new, we see the same results as the SBC. Thankfully, there are a few (and far between) elders and/or older males who seem to be much more in touch with the grassroots membership.

The most important action taken by Warren came in the form of an apology to women for his past views and the actions (or lack thereof) as a result. It is an apology worth including here, and with Rick, I offer the same apology to my sisters in Christ. As in other similar situations, I finally figured out areas where I was wrong, but it took too long, and thus my lack of change had negative effects for too long. In the following words, I believe Rick Warren speaks for many of us male church leaders.

> I PUBLICLY APOLOGIZE to every good woman in my life, church, and ministry that I failed to speak up for in my years of ignorance. What grieves me is that I hindered them in obeying the Great Commission command (and Acts 2:17–18) that EVERYONE is to TEACH in the church. I held them back from using the spiritual gifts and leadership skills that the Holy Spirit had sovereignly placed in them. That breaks my heart now, and I am truly repentant and sorry for my sin. I wish I could do it all over. Christian women, will you please forgive me? Regardless of attacks and the vote result, I want a clear conscience before my Master…that I repented, and that this sinner did what he asked me to do. With that I am completely content to let Him be the judge and evaluator of my life and ministry. We must live for an Audience of One.[8]

Similar updates keep coming and will no doubt continue. On June 26, 2023, the North Carolina-based Elevation Church notified Southern Baptist Conference leaders that they are ending their

---

8. Rick Warren, https://twitter.com/RickWarren/status/1667620086251925505?lang=en.

affiliation with the SBC. Elevation is one of the largest churches in this organization, with 19 campuses and a total weekly attendance of approximately 26,000. When two of the largest and best-known churches like Saddleback and Elevation leave at about the same time, a precedent is set that will likely prove to be the tip of the iceberg.

Restoration Church History

While it will be quite interesting to watch current history develop in evangelical churches, those of us in the Restoration heritage have some interesting history of our own. What is called the Restoration Movement (RM) had its beginning in the US during the late 1700s and early 1800s, with Alexander Campbell and Barton W. Stone serving as the best-known leaders. (The RM is often referred to as the Stone-Campbell Movement.) They and their followers viewed the Protestant Reformation Movement as having failed in key ways to unite Christianity when breaking away from the Catholic Church. Hence, they favored the term "restoration." Rather than trying to *reform* an existing church, they sought to *restore* the original church by going back to the Bible alone without written creeds that had defined many Protestant denominations.

While this sounded like a noble goal, the Restoration Movement adapted an approach to interpreting the Bible now called "pattern theology," or "blueprint theology." This strict approach of trying to interpret Scripture by taking the most literal views possible as a pattern to uphold led to an almost unbelievable number of divisions. When contextual and cultural factors are not taken into significant account, literalism will result in forms of legalism that stifle or prohibit practicing what Paul advocated in the 1 Corinthians 9 passage quoted earlier. The Christian Church and the Churches of Christ, including the International Churches of Christ, have as their foundation the Restoration Movement with all its strengths and weaknesses.

Contrary to popular belief, within much of the RM women

were not nearly as restricted in their church activities in earlier years as they came to be more recently. One of my favorite books on this subject, *Women Serving God,*[9] by John Mark Hicks, contains a section entitled "Historical Awareness." In this section, Hicks includes many references and quotes from the early twentieth century showing that women in the Churches of Christ were accorded many opportunities to speak publicly in church services. Some of these sources quoted were from the most conservative church leaders, which surprised me, especially as a former teacher of Restoration History in a ministry training school. Here is a good summary from Hicks:

> In the nineteenth century, it was not uncommon for women to participate in prayer and exhortation when assembled as a church (though unacceptable to Campbell and his son-in-law Pendleton, the editors of the *Millennial Harbinger):*

> > Not one scripture precept can be found against women taking part in social prayer and exhortation," wrote Faurot in 1866, "that does not equally forbid her singing." He reported that he only knew of "two congregations outside of Bethany, that did not allow women to all acts of religious worship," especially exhortation. "Who shall deny her," Faurot asked, "the privilege of praising her Lord, and speaking of his goodness to her?"[10]

ICOC History

The International Churches of Christ is a young movement, the RM stream of which I am a part, and has gone through several phases historically dating back to the 1970s. What I call

---

9. John Mark Hicks, *Women Serving God: My Journey in Understanding Their Story in the Bible* (Nashville, TN: JMH, 2020).

10. John Mark Hicks, *Women Serving God: My Journey in Understanding Their Story in the Bible* (Nashville, TN: JMH, 2020), 48. Kindle.

the Campus Ministry Movement phase had its beginning at the Crossroads Church of Christ in Gainesville, Florida. An earlier ministry, called Bible Chairs, focused on campus ministry and played its part, but the most dramatic results of growth came from Crossroads. The concepts of evangelistic small group Bible studies (initially called "soul talks") in informal settings, especially on the campus of the University of Florida, prayer partners (later termed discipling partners), and other activities led to rapid growth as hundreds of college students were baptized. The practice of couples leading campus ministries began, which was a bold step forward for women although their focus of leadership was limited to other women, and the women were not paid. In the early years, only the men were paid, but the wife's leadership was expected. A few women, called "Women's Counselors," were paid. Their focus was on women's ministry, but since they were not trained counselors in psychology, the titles changed to women's ministry leaders. Compared to more traditional Churches of Christ, this was indeed a big step forward for women.

By the time we reached the "Boston Movement" phase, church plantings added to rapid growth internationally, and for a period the growth was nothing short of amazing. Aside from these innovations mentioned, our worship settings were still patterned mainly after the more traditional churches, which included singing without the use of instrumental music and women serving only in the children's ministry and singing along with the congregation in worship services. Outside of these public settings, women did often participate in praying as a part of prayer circles in small groups. Otherwise, their roles were much more limited until the mid-1990s.

At this point, discussions began concerning how women could serve in more obvious ways. After all, many wives were on the ministry staff of churches along with their husbands. In another article I wrote several years ago, I described the changes that occurred during that time. Douglas Jacoby wrote an article or two that encapsulated these discussions. I presented a similar lesson in the Boston Garden to the whole Boston church, which was followed by a presentation by Kay McKean, the congregational women's ministry leader at the time. As I recall, Douglas' teaching addressed three topics: social drinking in moderation, women's roles, and the use of instrumental music in worship. Mine addressed only the role of women in the church.

Broader opportunities for our female members resulted from those discussions and lessons. I might mention that these discussions continued in different places over time before they were generally accepted. This acceptance resulted in women baptizing other women, serving as ushers, passing communion and contribution trays, singing on stage along with men, and sharing with men in giving welcomes, making announcements, and sharing testimonies in communion talks. They also shared alongside their husbands in parenting and marriage workshops. The women were required to always be accompanied by a man, even if he were only there in silence to "represent headship," as some term it. It has remained verboten in most of our churches for a woman to go on stage and lead any aspect of a service unaccompanied by a male. For the last 30 years, the majority of our churches have remained stuck in this place.

A Growing Pragmatism

However, we have not been as stuck as most assume. A growing number of church leaderships are daring to cross the virtual line in the sand on these issues, thankfully. In another article I wrote, "Male/Female Role Relationships in the Church" (in two parts),[11] I discussed the concept of natural evolution in both thinking and practice as we mature in Christ. Change sometimes occurs under the banner of common sense in ways that I believe God intends

---

11. Gordon Ferguson, "Male/Female Relationships in the Church," Gordon Ferguson Teaching Ministry, https://gordonferguson.org/male-female-role-relationships-in-the-church/.

and directs.

In Part 1 of that article, I quoted this passage and made some pertinent observations about the women's role. "All of us, then, who are mature should take such a view of things. And if on some point you think differently that too God will make clear to you. Only let us live up to what we have already attained" (Philippians 3:15–16). This passage promises that God will continue to reveal the practical application of his truths and keep us on a maturing track if we will cooperate by doing our best with what we know in the meantime. In both cases, time is necessary to produce a better understanding of certain things. Thus, an element of pragmatism is built into the Christian system by God himself.

To illustrate this principle, I shared the example of co-teaching a class in a leadership conference back in 2016 with Linda Brumley, who is a gifted teacher. The topic assigned to us was about forgiveness, and since Linda had recently published a book on the topic, I merely introduced the class and sat down. She taught the class. The class was excellent as well as entertaining, and no one covered their ears or walked out. It just seemed natural and didn't raise the hackles of anyone in the class, all of whom were ministry staff, both men and women. I don't believe for a moment that we violated any scripture, and I believe this will become clear in the next chapters of this book as we dig into the biblical passages that address the topic. I think everyone in that class simply saw the principle in Philippians 3 being carried out.

The fact that many would be reasonably comfortable with a woman teaching in this setting yet not in a Sunday service shows just how deeply embedded is our pattern theology. The next chapter of this book directly addresses this literalistic approach to interpretation and exposes its fallacies. It seems clear that women prophets were teaching in a Sunday service, based on 1 Corinthians 11. Yet we have made our own patterns, supposedly based on the early church pattern (which isn't actually there). For us, a common pattern looks something like this: three songs and a welcome, two more songs and communion, one song and the sermon, announcements, and a final song. At least that would be a recognizable "pattern" to many, or something quite similar and usually quite repetitious. But we appear to be very uncomfortable with the idea of allowing a female prophet to get factored into our patterns, 1 Corinthians 11 notwithstanding.

Stepping Up the Pace

Five years ago, my good friend Jeanie Shaw introduced a much broader view of women in the church with her book, *The View from Paul's Window,* addressing Paul's teaching on women. Although the book wasn't published until 2020, two years prior she sent electronic copies to many leaders whose opinions she valued. Most of them were immediately very positive in their support of her conclusions. I was not among them. I had a very negative reaction initially and wrote a very negative review of the book via email, strong enough to make me suspect it could seriously damage our otherwise very close relationship.

Fairly soon after sending my negative review, I went to Boston to visit Jeanie's husband, Wyndham, who was slowly dying of a terrible debilitating disease (MSA). He was my all-time best friend, but Jeanie was in my best friend category in her own right. When she and I started discussing her book, she was who she always is—a very calm, intelligent, spiritual disciple of Jesus. She apparently wasn't too disturbed by my review and just started asking questions that made me think. From that first discussion in person, my thinking began to undergo a metamorphosis. The male chauvinistic roots of my Louisiana upbringing, combined with my strongly hierarchical biblical training and experience, began to lose their grip on my entrenched dogmatism. In brief, I started thinking outside my own "box" and allowed myself to reconsider my long-cherished opinions. As the old humorous saying puts it, I no longer felt that I had the truth in a wee small box and had the key to all of the locks!

Like studying many other topics through the years, once I started examining the Bible without my "glasses" with preconceptions activated, I started seeing what I had missed. I have always loved truth and the concept of truth, knowing that Satan is the father of lies. Once enough pieces of a puzzle start fitting together, the big picture doesn't lag far behind. Thus it was with me on this topic. I wrote those two website articles shortly afterwards, and in rereading them recently, I was struck with how fast I assimilated that big picture. I have read multiple books and articles since then, but I'm still good with what I wrote at a much earlier stage. Once we are able to shed our traditional presuppositions, the topic becomes simpler.

Jeanie's writing and teaching on the topic was not received so warmly by some, and she received significant resistance, causing her to delay publication for several years. During the delay, she continued to receive very positive commendations from not a few well-known, highly respected leaders. Steve Kinnard, a highly recognized teacher among us, wrote the foreword for the book, and his first comment to me about the book sums it up well. He simply said, "I loved the book."

That was a common opinion about the book, and despite the limited pockets of resistance, she undoubtedly has ushered in a change of thinking well beyond just mine. Although the tide on this issue is turning for many, not all have turned (nor will they). However, I do believe God used the controversy over the book to raise much greater awareness than if it had been quietly published. God has a sense of timing, always.

Jeanie recently completed her doctoral dissertation addressing pattern theology and various ways it affects our spiritual formation. I believe this study may have a greater impact on our study of the topic than her first one. Although my next chapter is not nearly as in depth as Jeanie's newest book on Restoration hermeneutics,[12]

---

12. Jeanie Shaw, *Re-Examining Our Lenses: The Relationship Between Restoration Movement Hermeneutics and Spiritual Formation* (Spring, TX: Theatron, 2024).

it will prove helpful in providing my readers some background about the brand of biblical interpretation (hermeneutics) that we usually term "pattern" or "blueprint theology." Those of us in Restoration churches are heavily influenced by this interpretative approach, whether we recognize it or not. As you read chapter two, some light bulbs are sure to start appearing in your mind.

Keeping an Open Mind

By this point, many of you reading thus far have either come into the study of the topic with preconceived ideas, perhaps conclusory ones, or you have begun leaning strongly in one direction or the other. You are most likely identifying with the side of the egalitarians or that of the complementarians. That is natural. If you do see yourself on the complementarian side, I'm just reminding you of the value of always keeping an open mind.

One thing that is very interesting and very puzzling at the same time is how we respond to recognized scholarship. I have heard many serious students of the Bible in our family of churches praise N.T. Wright as the most outstanding New Testament scholar in the world. There can be no doubt that he is the most recognized expert on Paul. I have owned one book on Paul by him, a biography, for a number of years.[13] It is a substantial book of over 400 pages. A friend of mine attended a lecture by Wright and purchased two of his books on *Paul and the Faithfulness of God,* each of which combines two volumes into one. The first book of two parts is 600 pages long, and the second book of two parts is 1650 pages long. Both of these books are inscribed to me and signed by the author, by the way. Nice!

No doubt he is an expert on all things Pauline. Although he doesn't like the terms often used to describe the two main views of women's roles, feeling that they are too polarizing, his own views would place him in the egalitarian side. I use quotes from him later

---

13. Tom Wright, *Paul: A Biography* (NY: HarperOne, 2018).

in this book that make this point. Yet, many who praise his scholarship generally reject his views of women in ministry. As I said, interesting and puzzling at the same time.

When I was cutting my teeth in formal theological studies over a half century ago the recognized Pauline expert in that era was F.F. Bruce (1910–1990). I read with great interest an account that relates directly to our topic at hand. Scot McKnight described a meal he had at the home of F.F. Bruce while doing his doctoral studies. During a very long conversation prior to the meal itself, Scot had a question in mind to ask Bruce, and his account of the question and answer is as follows:

> "Professor Bruce, what do you think of women's ordination?" "I don't think the New Testament talks about ordination," he replied. "What about the silencing passages of Paul on women?" I asked. "I think Paul would roll over in his grave if he knew we were turning his letters into torah." Wow! I thought. That's a good point to think about. Thereupon I asked a question that he answered in such a way that it reshaped my thinking: "What do you think, then, about women in church ministries?" Professor Bruce's answer was as Pauline as Paul was: "I'm for whatever God's Spirit grants women's gifts to do." So am I. Let the blue parakeets sing![14]

When two of the most recognized specialists on Paul and his writing agree on such an important subject, I say we ought to at least give an ear and careful consideration to what they, and others who agree with them, have to say on the subject.

---

14. Scot McKnight, *The Blue Parakeet, 2nd Ed: Rethinking How You Read the Bible* (Grand Rapids, MI: Zondervan, 2028), 261. Kindle.

Chapter 2

A Hermeneutical Perspective: Digging Out the Roots of Pattern Theology

I n Chapter 1, I briefly explained the history of what is called the Restoration Movement. Basically, this was a valiant effort, complete with good intentions, to succeed in doing what the Reformation Movement (Protestantism) had failed to do. Both movements were dedicated to going back to Scripture as the sole guide for Christianity, *Sola Scriptura,* rather than continuing to follow the man-made traditions of the Catholic Church. However, Protestantism became divided quickly and deeply in spite of those good intentions, splintering into about 150 different groups by the 1700s. It was not unheard of for people to lose their lives at the hands of those who differed from them doctrinally. Study the life of John Calvin or the Anabaptist Movement, and you will see that I am not exaggerating. Although nothing was humorous about the actual facts involved, the following little story humorously describes the reality and nature of those divisions.

I was walking across a bridge one day and I saw a man about to jump. I said, 'Stop, don't do it.' 'Why shouldn't I?' he asked. 'Well, are you a Christian?' I asked. He said: 'Yes.' I said, 'Me too. Are you Catholic or Protestant?' 'Protestant.' 'Me too. Are you Episcopalian or Baptist?' 'Baptist.' 'Wow, me too. Are you Baptist church of God or Baptist church of the Lord?' 'Baptist Church of God.' 'Me too. Are you original Baptist Church of God or are you reformed Baptist Church of God?' 'Reformed.' 'Me too. Are you Reformed Baptist Church of God, reformation of 1879, or Reformed Baptist Church of God, reformation of 1915?' He said, 'Reformation of 1915.' I said: 'Die, heretic scum,' and pushed him off.[15]

A Logical Approach that Wasn't

In looking at the goals of the Restoration Movement, the chief of which was a Bible-based unity, much of what was said in the early stages sounded both noble and logical. But logic is tricky business. What appears to be totally logical to one person can seem illogical to another person. We all come to the Bible with our interpretative "glasses" on, usually not knowing that they are there. Many things shape how we see through those lenses. None of us ever arrives at the goal of perfect interpretation of the Bible, much less perfect application of it in our lives. But try we must, trusting that the real salvation issues can be understood and followed by those with good hearts who are seeking to love and serve God.

In the mind of the most influential early restoration leader, Alexander Campbell, logic could lead us to that desired correct interpretation. Here is how I described him in the second edition of my book, *Prepared to Answer*, in chapter 9 on "Restoration Churches."

> Alexander Campbell, the most influential thinker in the movement, had been deeply influenced by rational philosophers of the Enlightenment, like John Locke, who believed everything could be reduced to a set of facts. Applying Lockean philosophy to the Bible, Campbell viewed the New Testament as a pattern, comparing it to the pattern which God gave to the Jews for the construction of the tabernacle.[16]

---

15. Emo Phillips, *The Guardian*, Sept 29, 2005, https://www.theguardian.com/stage/2005/sep/29/comedy.religion.
16. Gordon Ferguson, *Prepared to Answer: Restoring Truth in an Age of Relativism* (Spring, TX: Illumination Publsihers, 2009), 114.

The Bible does use the term "pattern" in describing God's directions to Moses regarding building the tabernacle to exact specifications. From this came the idea that if the Old Covenant was to be followed carefully and precisely, how much more should those of us under the New Covenant do the same? That sounds logical, right? However, the Old Testament clearly demonstrated that we could not follow anything closely enough to be saved by our obedience. "For the law was given through Moses; grace and truth came through Jesus Christ" (John 1:17). Or as Peter put it in Acts 15:10, the Law was a "yoke that neither we nor our ancestors have been able to bear." The very concept of the Restoration Movement led to legalism quickly, becoming a very doctrinally focused movement which became far more legalistic with the passing of years.

Translations of the New Testament Didn't Help

In what we call the Pastoral Epistles (1 & 2 Timothy and Titus), Paul addresses numerous false teachings. He informed his younger proteges how to handle these teachings and those who taught them. One of the unfortunate translations of terminology found often in these three letters to evangelists paved the way to an increasing emphasis on what we often call "doctrinal matters" or "theological matters." I refer to the term *sound doctrine*. This very theologically sounding term became one of the most used when debating what should and shouldn't be a part of the pattern to follow. Debates in print and in person were in vogue as leaders argued about various aspects of the so-called "pattern," hence the term "pattern theology."

If one sees sound doctrine as strict adherence to all theological doctrines in the New Testament, matters of interpretation become more of a focus than Jesus or the Christian life. Here are a few passages from the Pastoral letters using this term, taken here from the *New American Standard Bible,* one of the most accurate translations from Greek to English (with emphases added).

1 Timothy 4:6
In pointing out these things to the brethren, you will be
a good servant of Christ Jesus, constantly nourished on
the words of the faith and of the *sound doctrine* which
you have been following.

2 Timothy 4:3
For the time will come when they will not endure *sound
doctrine;* but wanting to have their ears tickled, they will
accumulate for themselves teachers in accordance to
their own desires,

Titus 1:9
holding fast the faithful word which is in accordance
with the teaching, so that he will be able both to exhort
in *sound doctrine* and to refute those who contradict.

Why is this translation both inaccurate and misleading? The
word translated "sound," *hugiainô,* is translated every time in the
Pastorals this way in the NASB, and yet the word itself means
"healthy." Hence, sound teaching is teaching that makes one spiritually healthy. It is translated better in other passages. For example, here are two, also from the NASB.

Luke 5:31
And Jesus answered and said to them, "It is not those who
are *well* who need a physician, but those who are sick."

3 John 1:2
Beloved, I pray that in all respects you may prosper and
be in *good health,* just as your soul prospers.

The word "doctrine," *didaskalia,* is translated as such 9 of 15 times in the Pastorals in the NASB. *The Cambridge English Dictionary* defines doctrine as "a belief or set of beliefs, especially political or religious ones, that are taught and accepted by a particular group." When you are indoctrinated with an approach to interpretation with its foundation in pattern theology, sound doctrine will come to mean a type of important or essential theological doctrines, and much will fall into the category of salvation essentials. When doctrine is exalted to such a status, it can be shocking to see what will be included under the banner of salvation matters. It is, in fact, quite shocking when you study the history of the RM. But this word "doctrine" in the Greek is simply the normal word for teaching. Sound doctrine is healthy teaching, no more and no less.

Pattern Theology Briefly Explained

Pattern theology begins with the premise that precision obedience can save or damn, thus correct interpretation becomes all important. How do we know what is a part of the pattern of sound doctrine? How does the Bible teach us? In the mainstream Churches of Christ, I was taught that the pattern of sound doctrine is determined in four basic ways.

1. **Statement of fact:** Anything stated as fact is to be taken at literal face value. This is most often true, although not always. Satan's lies are stated by him as fact. Hyperbole (overstatement to make a point) was often used by Jesus but wasn't meant to be taken literally, or else we would be plucking out our eyeballs and cutting off our hands (Matthew 18:8–9). I roll my eyes as I recall teaching in various settings in which the one teaching said repeatedly, "Well, it says what it means and means what it says."

2. **Direct command:** If the early church was given a direct command by inspired apostles and prophets, it was meant to be included as a continual part of the pattern. Thus, the

commands for women to keep silent in church (1 Corinthians 14:34) and not to teach or have any authority over a man (1 Timothy 2:12) are to be taken literally and for all time. (I am tempted to add here, "and context be damned.")

3. **Approved apostolic example:** If the inspired apostles and those led by them did something, then what they did was to be the pattern that we should imitate. This supposed way of teaching us the "pattern" was nothing if not highly dangerous and damaging. I will further elaborate on this, for my own background shows its uncertainty of application and its path into folly.

4. **Necessary inference:** Since the church in Corinth was to collect a financial offering on every first day of the week (1 Corinthians 16:1–2), we should necessarily infer that this is a part of the pattern for us also. Most of us haven't stopped to think that this particular occurrence was in connection with an offering for needy disciples in Jerusalem, as were all specific church offerings found in the New Testament. We do not find any example of how they collected money for local needs beyond that, but we ride merrily along with our long-standing necessary inference as we pass the offering plate weekly (or send it in online these days).

If you think logically about the New Testament teaching us in these four ways so that we might find and follow the accurate pattern, all four practically boil down into one—approved apostolic example. We simply follow the example of the early church in what they were told and in what they did. But questions abound! Are those statements of fact really for all of us for all time? Are those commands directed at all of us for all time? Which apostolic examples are approved and who does the approving and by what means? How do we know that certain things are to be necessarily inferred by all of us for all time? Questions like these can be multiplied almost to infinity.

Painful Real-Life Examples

I don't have to conjure these up or look for them, as I grew up with them. My first experience in the church was with what was called a "one-cup, no Sunday school" Church of Christ. I tell about this painful experience in my book, *My Three Lives.*[17] When Jesus instituted the "Lord's Supper" at the Passover Meal with the apostles, it says that he took "the cup," not "the cups." Thus, in the church of my youth, we had one cup that was passed around to every person. Certain interesting memories come to mind. The first grows out of my current focus on speaking and writing on racial issues, especially involving Blacks and Whites.

I remember visiting a church on Easter Sunday when I was 15 years old that was large for that particular odd fellowship. It was a large all-White church, since almost all churches of any denomination were either all-White or all-Black in 1957. Just before services began, a nicely dressed Black woman came in and sat right in the middle aisle between the two sections, in the back row. Since the pews were full and White folks were racially tilted, a chair was set up for her there. This meant that half the church would drink from the same large cup of grape juice that she had drunk from. I can't know what was in people's minds and wasn't situated to watch who of those on that side drank or didn't drink from the cup after she had, but my imagination never let me forget the moment or the questions it prompted in me.

I remember a story told by a fellow preacher when I was a young preacher and no longer a one-cupper. He said that he too was raised in the same type of church I had been raised in and their one cup doctrine got severely tested when his uncle developed tuberculosis. He said that they became a two-cup church quickly,

---

17. Gordon Ferguson, *My Three Lives: A Story of One Man and Three Movements* (Spring, TX: Illumination Publishers, 2016).

one for his uncle and one for everyone else. But it does say that Jesus took THE cup after all, doesn't it? There were those among us who believed this to be a salvation issue, hence using multiple cups would send you to hell.

I could elaborate on the no-Sunday School part, or the six-months debate which ensued when we decided to switch from un-fermented grape juice to wine to attract an additional family to our church who were driving a long way to have wine in communion. Most of you reading this would have a difficult time even believing the nature and number of issues like these that led to divisions and separate fellowships, most of which had their own publication to keep them unified among themselves.

I saw one list with an even one hundred separate fellowships, all claiming to be Churches of Christ and all claiming to be the only ones following the pattern that led to heaven. One friend told me that his church believed that only one other church in the US besides his was following the correct pattern as they were, so since they couldn't "forsake the assembly" (Hebrews 10:25) even when on vacation, they were limited to one place to spend their vacations—the city with the other "faithful" church in it. He said that his group got the best of the deal, because their one sister church was in California and the California faithful were stuck spending their vacations in his city, a not-so-nice one.

Why Are We Talking About Such Nonsense?

That is precisely what some (many) of you are thinking about now, right? Easy answer. This type of biblical interpretation is not just in our history, it's in our DNA. We may not know it is there, but trust me, it is. In fact, when we are studying the topic of women and their roles in the church, pattern theology is front and center, right at the head of the line. In spite of everything that has been said and written about women in the Old Testament and in the New Testament, patriarchy has thus far still won the day in our church circles. This term and its implications will be described more fully in the next chapter, but its basic definition is that of male power and domination. Elements of it have been weakened in many other ways in the secular world. Women can now vote, but suffrage was neither a short nor an easy battle. Study US history to see what a long and fairly recent battle that was. Women can now hold political office. Women can now be in managerial positions in companies with authority over male employees. In the world outside the church, women can do whatever men can do, period.

That doesn't mean that sexism isn't real in 2024 as I write this, for it is. We could talk about equal opportunities, equal pay, and a whole host of related items to show its continued existence. I am not saying that everything the world does should become our "pattern," not by a long shot, but I am saying that the actual teaching of the New Testament viewed through genuinely accepted principles of hermeneutics should determine what we accept and reject. I believe we have allowed our patriarchy DNA plus our pattern theology DNA to prejudice us against women and against biblical truth, despite our denials and blindness to those facts. I believe it will change in the church, although probably not until my generation and at least one below me dies out. It feels sad to me that I won't live to see women doing what they should already be doing in the church. I would love to hear a woman preach a Sunday sermon just once before I die.

Patterns, Seen and Unseen, that We Ignore

When I was experiencing my indoctrination as a young man into the strange maze of pattern theology, I remember being taught that there were five biblically designated acts of worship to be observed in Sunday services. These were singing, praying, preaching, communion, and giving. Each of the five could be "proved" to be not only allowable, but absolutely essential. I recall one very influential editor of one of our most popular periodicals saying that not only were they a necessary part of our Sunday worship services, but they could not be mixed or combined;

they had to remain separate. Hence, for example, no singing was allowed while the collection plates were being passed.

As we have hopefully established, everything that the early church did was never intended to be a pattern for all times, including our time. Yet, we are still unduly influenced by some early church examples and oddly, not influenced by others. These practices were often begun during the early RM days for the purpose of trying to follow a pattern, and we simply continue to follow them out of tradition. Rarely do we stop to think about why we do it, nor do we think about how we follow some examples and ignore others. We have morphed into a strange blend of reasoning and traditions, it seems to me.

Our human biases have influenced us in ways that we may not have seen, but in ways that are actually predictable. Many examples of how the early church functioned we simply ignore and don't consider as examples, or patterns, that we must follow. Other examples we do follow and consider them very important and even essential. Those in this category, somewhat predictably, fall into two basic areas. One is money related, and the other is anything judged to affect women's roles in the church. But let's begin our journey by noting other examples that are clear, but we seem comfortable ignoring them as unimportant and certainly non-essential.

I will begin by looking at the type of church services described in 1 Corinthians 11 and 14. In these, a number of different people spoke, either by prophesying or by speaking in a foreign language with an interpreter nearby. To us, that isn't viewed as a pattern. We almost always have one preacher (a male) deliver one lesson for the entire teaching slot.

Further, many of the early disciples met in small groups, in the houses of disciples. In those cases, the house owner was likely one of the wealthier members with a larger house, but it was still a house church. You've read the verses. As we will later note in discussing Phoebe, rich people in the Roman Empire were expected to give money for the common good of the Empire and its citizens, just like many rich people do in our society. In Rome, they were called benefactors; in America, they are called philanthropists. Men like Bill Gates and Warren Buffett have given billions of dollars to charitable causes.

To most of us, especially leaders, the near exclusive format of house churches in the New Testament is decidedly not a pattern we think should be followed, and in many cases it has become a pattern to be rejected and spoken against. We have an active house church movement among us now, and it is not a popular movement among many of our leaders, for obvious reasons. If our larger churches start losing members to this increasingly popular trend, will we be able to continue functioning and supporting our ministry and administrative staff and the various works to which we are already committed financially?

To those who now meet almost exclusively in house church formats, you may be drawn to view this practice as a biblical pattern. The early church had little choice, for by the middle of the first century, Christianity was viewed by the Roman Empire as an illegal religion, *a religio illicita*. Church buildings began being built in the fourth century after the Emperor Constantine made Christianity the official religion of the empire. We can argue all we want about whether "big church" or "little church" (house church) is best, but it is a matter of preference and a matter of choice. There was never an intended pattern.

I was raised in what was essentially a house church, and it was an embarrassment to me since all of my friends went to large churches with nice buildings. When I became a part of a church that had meetings of both types, I had some emotional issues to deal with in becoming comfortable in a house church setting. My life was turned around for God in a big church setting, and I will never lose my love for meeting in that configuration. At the same time, my personal preference, based on many decades of experience, is to regularly meet in some combination of both configurations. But regardless of your preference, please avoid trying to make either type of meeting into a pattern supposedly based on the New Testament. We have been damaged quite enough by such erroneous views in Restoration churches.

Next, let's look at the pattern of church contributions found in the New Testament. As far as I see from specific examples, all of the collections mentioned were relief efforts for poor disciples who were facing hard times financially due to some type of unexpected emergency. That's true of the most profound in-depth passage on giving in the Bible, 2 Corinthians 8–9. Even the passage we use (as a pattern, by the way) to support weekly giving on Sundays is for this purpose. Read it.

1 Corinthians 16:1–3

¹Now about the collection for the Lord's people: Do what I told the Galatian churches to do. ² On the first day of every week, each one of you should set aside a sum of money in keeping with your income, saving it up, so that when I come no collections will have to be made. ³ Then, when I arrive, I will give letters of introduction to the men you approve and send them with your gift to Jerusalem.

I know that the early church did support some who served in the ministry, for Paul mentioned funds having been sent to him, for which he was most grateful. He also argued in 1 Corinthians 9 that ministers had a right to such support, although he refused that right with the Corinthian church for some reason not fully explained. He also made the case, in 1 Timothy 5, that elders who taught and preached had a right to financial support by the church. How they gathered such funds we are not told.

Only one time in the Bible was a collection gathered on the first day of the week, and that contribution was a collection being prepared during a specific period of time to send to Jerusalem.

Never say that pattern theology is not a part of our Restoration heritage. Sunday contributions were developed and based on that one example. I am fine with giving on Sunday and have done it for decades until online contributions became a desirable option due to my teaching ministry travel. But it doesn't have to be done in a specific way during a specific time. I just want to show that we do practice pattern theology by following some examples of the early church, but discount others with ease. We could mention other early church practices such as *agape* meals. 1 Corinthians 11 shows that the early church seemed to imitate Jesus' example of observing the communion during a regular meal. Most of us have never done that, unless perhaps when meeting in a house church setting.

Patterns Insisted Upon for Women!

Does it not strike you as extremely odd that we dismiss with ease many examples of how the early church functioned and worshipped, and yet insist that we follow a supposed pattern when women are involved? Having studied this topic so much, it doesn't strike me as odd at all, at least not in our present setting. Patriarchy, with its absolutely undeniable biases toward women, drives our strange inconsistencies which are also undeniable. And these inconsistencies can be seen readily in the very same chapter of the Bible. Let's read.

> **1 Corinthians 14:34**
> "Women should remain silent in the churches. They are not allowed to speak, but must be in submission, as the law says."

I can just picture someone from my past saying, "Yup—it says what it means and means what it says. Women just need to keep quiet except for singing." How many times have I heard that one? A lot! We will visit this verse in its context later, but I will mention now that the word "silent" (*sigao* in the Greek) used here means absolute silence, and that would preclude singing. But five verses later, we read this.

1 Corinthians 14:39
"Therefore, my brothers and sisters, be eager to prophesy, and do not forbid speaking in tongues."

Nope—we are definitely going to put the brakes on that business of women prophesying, and we are going to expressly *forbid* anyone to speak in tongues. That is not for our day, right? At this point, we become very anxious to look at the broad context of miraculous gifts to explain this one. It has to be interpreted in its first century context, we say. When women are involved, the only context that really matters is a very broad one extending all the way back to the introduction of patriarchy in Genesis 3:16. Let's keep going.

1 Corinthians 11:20–21
"So then, when you come together, it is not the Lord's Supper you eat, ^{21} for when you are eating, some of you go ahead with your own private suppers. As a result, one person remains hungry and another gets drunk."

The abuse of the Lord's Supper is described in 1 Corinthians 11, starting in verse 17 and going to the end of the chapter. Whatever else may be said, their communion took place within a sit-down meal, as it did at the Passover meal when Jesus instituted it. As stated earlier, we dismiss this example and don't come close to trying to find some pattern that we can use other than having the elements of bread and juice. Our modern setting is totally different. But we have no problem with that, since women are not involved in any type of leadership (except perhaps cooking those agape meals, the "love feast" as it came to be called). But in the earlier part of the same chapter, we are going to get our hermeneutical microscopes engaged and find a pattern to limit females. Just watch.

1 Corinthians 11:7–12

[7] A man ought not to cover his head, since he is the image and glory of God; but woman is the glory of man. [8] For man did not come from woman, but woman from man; [9] neither was man created for woman, but woman for man. [10] It is for this reason that a woman ought to have authority over her own head, because of the angels. [11] Nevertheless, in the Lord woman is not independent of man, nor is man independent of woman. [12] For as woman came from man, so also man is born of woman. But everything comes from God.

A Pattern of a Pattern

Just to make sure we have all of the support for our pattern of a pattern, let's include 1 Corinthians 11:3: "But I want you to realize that the head of every man is Christ, and the head of the woman is man, and the head of Christ is God." In the example of men not covering their heads, mentioned first, and the women covering hers, most of us relegate these regulations to the first century setting in Corinth and what such coverings or lack thereof implied in that particular cultural setting. Although my earliest years were spent attending a church in which women did follow that practice (yes, of course as a pattern), such a literal practice can hardly be found anywhere today.

But what can be found is another pattern, invented by us as a pattern of a pattern. Here is what I mean. Since women were to have a "sign" of authority on their heads, this should prove that women in front of the audience participating visibly and publicly should also have a sign of some sort to show that males are the head of females. I'm sorry, and I'm not wanting to be unnecessarily offensive here regarding the practices we have developed that are viewed as doctrinally essential, but this is one of the more nonsensical practices we have invented in the name of supposed biblical teaching. It has more holes in it than Swiss cheese.

For starters, although the older version of the NIV uses the phrase "sign of authority" in verse 10, notice that the 2011 NIV does not. It simply says, "have authority over her own head." The Greek Interlinear shows the exact words in their exact order in Greek. "Because of this ought the woman authority to have on the head because of the angels." Obviously, the newer NIV is the more accurate translation. Some have combined the idea of a visible sign with the idea of man being the head of woman and state this combination principle as "showing headship." A woman on stage (our terminology and practices would have seemed strange in those early house church settings) must by all means "show headship."

Next, notice that this "authority on the head" was because of the angels, not because of the presence of anyone who could be seen in their assemblies. And what in the world does it even mean anyway? You can find about as many explanations for this verse as for 1 Corinthians 15:29 and "baptism for the dead." How in the world can we take such an ambiguous passage as 1 Corinthians 11:10 and develop a practice that we boldly teach as a doctrinally accurate and essential one? It staggers the imagination (mine at least)!

Before I land this plane, some additional questions are in order. If a woman must have a visible sign to show her submission to man, why does a man not need some sort of visible sign to show his submission to Christ, who is his head? Further, why did Christ on earth not need some visible sign to show his submission to God, who is his head? Why is the woman singled out as the only one who must have a visible sign to show her submission in all cultural settings for all times? It appears that we have made an unending pattern of a pattern that had its roots in a first century, specific cultural setting alone.

So What Is Our Pattern of a Pattern?

Once we started allowing women to do things in our services beyond singing as part singers and ushering, it progressed to include her sharing her testimony as a part of a "communion talk." The man had to go first in introducing the communion part of the service and then introduce the woman who would then share her testimony. The man would close out by leading the prayer. In the earliest days of this practice, the woman was not to read Scripture or give a "word of instruction," for then she would be "teaching men," nor was she to lead the prayer, for that would be "leading men."

In time, some churches began allowing a woman to be alone on stage to make announcements or do the whole communion service, complete with ending in prayer. Some churches became so bold as to allow a woman to do the welcome alone and lead a song and perhaps even lead a prayer to close the entire worship service. During the pandemic, with our online services, I was surprised (delightfully so) to see these practices observed in several places.

But for those intent on having a visible sign of authority, thus showing the headship of the man, this presented a dilemma. A pattern was invented using a localized pattern from the first century as its basis. One solution employed by some was to allow a woman to do something alone on stage, but to have a man go up with her and stand to the side. I wonder what our female visitors thought of that one, or male visitors for that matter? I heard one presentation on this specific topic of the women's role in which this "man standing alone" was mentioned as an odd practice, although they had evidently practiced it previously. How did they propose to replace the oddity? By having a man *always* accompany the woman and take an active lead, after which she could then share her part of the activity. Does this not strike you as a step backward for women?

In this same presentation, which had me scratching my head a number of times, the question of whether a woman could lead singing was answered thusly. "No, for her demeanor would violate headship." Head-scratching time again. What about her demeanor would be a violation of headship? Maybe waving her arms in directing the tempo of the song? If that was the supposed violation, would it not then be wrong for a prophetess to gesture as she prophesied and gave a "word of instruction" (1 Corinthians 11:5, 14:6)? Announcing the song would surely be less invasive to showing headship than giving a word of instruction as a female prophet.

I could go on here with many other illustrations of how our movement of churches has summarily dismissed some "patterns" or examples of how the early church functioned and yet has found a way to make other practices into a pattern today. We could include contributions as a part of a Sunday service, communion every Sunday (based on Acts 20 and some assumed "necessary inferences" from that passage), Sunday and midweek services being a "meeting of the body," where the limitations for women are more strict than other meetings of the same people, and on we go.

A Final Observation

I don't doubt anyone's good intentions, nor do I doubt those of the early Jews who developed what they supposed were ways to protect the stipulations of the Law itself. Erecting protective "fences" doesn't protect; they double the stipulations and complicate what should have been far simpler and far better. But traditions have a way of becoming exalted to the same level as Scripture, and we know what Jesus had to say about such a process and result in Matthew 15.

The New Testament, when *not* seen as a pattern, provides us many freedoms to develop approaches to "doing church" in ways that fit our particular culture. But the heavy hand of patriarchy with its unending march toward power and control is the retaining wall blocking true freedom. The old saying that we all have much to learn is undoubtedly true, but another stark truth is that we also have much to unlearn. That is the challenge we face in biblical hermeneutics, and few areas of learning and unlearning seem more of a challenge than observing the true gender equality that Jesus observed, and that we should observe. May God help us!

Chapter 3

An Old Testament Perspective:
Back to the Beginning

Now that we have covered a historical perspective and a hermeneutical (the way we interpret Scripture) perspective, we are better prepared to begin dealing with the biblical perspective of our topic. Specifically, I will examine in some detail two passages in the Old Testament, followed by an examination of three in the New Testament in later chapters. Following those, a subsequent chapter will include references to and observations about the many specific women whose examples speak clearly, if we are listening, in both the Old and New Testaments. Chapter eight will address a topic that in spite of its importance, is rarely, if ever, discussed in books like this one about women and their roles.

As we conduct this examination of an Old Testament perspective, we will explore together the broad assumption that has become the basis for multiple other incorrect assumptions and denials of other truths. While the details involved will not be dealt with to an exhaustive extent, nor will all of the complexities involved, none of these discussions of Old Testament passages will be either simplistic or short. It is a complex topic, and it is a controversial topic. As mentioned in my introduction, my view of a teacher's role is that we should carefully study complex topics and then present them in a way that neither compromises truth nor confuses the average listener or reader. With that as my goal, let's jump into this part of our study.

The Genesis of Bad Theology

Genesis 2:18 (NASB)
Then the LORD God said, "It is not good for the man to be alone; I will make him a helper suitable for him."

Before we delve into the meaning of, and mistaken assumptions about this text, let's first examine the context of Genesis 1 and 2. Note that a misinterpretation of this verse is the beginning point of faulty, dangerous theology. Now, imagine that you were a first-time reader of the Bible and an avid student of literature, beginning with absolutely no preconceptions. What would you see in these first two chapters of the Bible? You would see God speak the world into existence *ex nihilo* (out of nothing), as Hebrews 11:3, Psalms 33:6–9, and many other passages state. On the sixth day of creation, the climax was reached with the creation of human beings in the very image of God.

Genesis 1:26–31 (NASB)
[26] Then God said, "Let Us make man in Our image, according to Our likeness; and let them rule over the fish of the sea and over the birds of the sky and over the cattle and over all the earth, and over every creeping thing that creeps on the earth." [27] God created man in His own image, in the image of God He created him; male and female He created them. [28] God blessed them; and God said to them, "Be fruitful and multiply, and fill the earth, and subdue it; and rule over the fish of the sea and over the birds of the sky and over every living thing that moves on the earth." [29] Then God said, "Behold, I have given you every plant yielding seed that is on the surface of all the earth, and every tree which has fruit yielding seed; it shall be food for you; [30] and to every beast of the earth and to every bird of the sky and to everything that

moves on the earth which has life, *I have given* every green plant for food"; and it was so. [31] God saw all that He had made, and behold, it was very good. And there was evening and there was morning, the sixth day.

Prior to the creation of humans, as God systematically brought order out of disorder, he pronounced that it was good. After he had created a male and female, humankind, he said that it was very good. This gives us a hint of how significant it was for God to create others in his own image. It was, as we will see, of huge significance. Note what is stated about male and female as a pair, as a team. They were to rule over all living creatures—fish, birds, cattle, creeping things, every living thing moving on the earth. They were to have children and fill the earth with other humans, subduing the earth.

Male and female together were to accomplish all of this as a team. There is in the creative account absolutely no hint that the male would have any sort of dominion over the female, but rather that both would have dominion over the earth and all other life on it. The only thing discovered in the text by this point is total equality between male and female. Nothing more, nothing less. Mutuality is perhaps a preferred term, for equality can signify too much independence rather than cooperation in accomplishing common goals.

The *Imago Dei*—Made in God's Image

Male and female were made in the image of God, the *Imago Dei*—a huge event with huge implications. It ties in directly to the statement in Genesis 2:18 that it wasn't good for the man to be alone. Whether he was lonely or not, as is usually assumed, we are not told in the text. But without woman, the man was incomplete for the purposes God had in creating humankind in the first place. Together, they were representatives of the image of God. It took both, but why?

One, it takes two people to make kids and populate the earth, which was a stated purpose in Genesis 1. Through this, we have God as the Creator of humanity joined by humans in what is called, appropriately, procreation. We do our part in this way and in many other ways to reflect God's creativity.

Two, the task of subduing and ruling the earth was also a task for male and female teamwork. The Holy Spirit brought order out of chaos to the point that humankind could take over their part. That is what the text says.

Three, and here we enter deeper concepts, humans at their best are but a dim reflection of God. Adam alone was an incomplete *imago Dei*. Although God is described with the masculine pronoun, he is neither male nor female. Some descriptions denote female attributes.[18] He is God. It is often said that God, and then the earthly Jesus, demonstrate all the best qualities of both male and female. Perhaps wisdom in Proverbs is identified as feminine to help provide this balance. Adam alone was an incomplete image bearer of Deity through masculinity alone. Femininity was missing from the needed equation until Eve was added.

Four, since God is a triune being, consisting of the Father, Son, and Holy Spirit, God is, by definition, relational within himself. Thus, Adam alone could not be the representation of the relational nature of God without a companion.

Five, and this point may be the most significant of all—Adam alone could not accomplish the human role in the universal spiritual battle for which God created humans to engage. Two humans, male and female constituting humankind, even in their initial perfection and sinlessness still failed, but there was something about this battle that is far bigger than we might think. Somehow, the creation of humans in God's image had a highly significant part in the spiritual battle that has been raging for God knows how long (and only he knows how long).

---

18. See Deut 32:11; Ps 22:9–10, 71:6; Is 49:15, 66:9,13; Lk 13:34, 15:8–10.

If we are paying attention when we read the Bible, this galactic spiritual warfare jumps off the page time and time again, sometimes in shocking ways. Ephesians 6:12 states the principle well: "For our struggle is not against flesh and blood, but against the rulers, against the authorities, against the powers of this dark world and against the spiritual forces of evil in the heavenly realms." Paul speaks here of spiritual battle, not simply about earthly political and national leaders, but rather those in the heavenly realms who operate through worldly systems and structures (like nations, cultures, societal structures, etc.). Because these evil spiritual forces work through those human systems, there is such a mutuality and overlap that it is often difficult to make a distinction. From time to time, God pulls back the curtain between the physical and spiritual universes to let us see something of this battle. Think of Job for starters. God allowed Satan amazing liberties in attacking Job's family and Job himself. God was placing a huge bet on Job's spirituality, and Satan was betting against him and bringing everything he had against Job in the wager. We begin to see that far more is at stake than we usually stop to contemplate between the forces of good and the forces of evil.

You perhaps recall the early morning exchange between Elisha and his servant in 2 Kings 6.

2 Kings 6:15–17

[15] When the servant of the man of God got up and went out early the next morning, an army with horses and chariots had surrounded the city. "Oh no, my lord! What shall we do?" the servant asked. [16] "Don't be afraid," the prophet answered. "Those who are with us are more than those who are with them." [17] And Elisha prayed, "Open his eyes, LORD, so that he may see." Then the LORD opened the servant's eyes, and he looked and saw the hills full of horses and chariots of fire all around Elisha.

This is such an exciting story, and I encourage you to read the rest of it. Don't ever try to tell me that God doesn't have a sense of humor! (Where do you think we got ours?)

Perhaps the most shocking account showing the intensity of the spiritual battle taking place is found in Daniel 9 and 10. Chapter 9 begins with Daniel praying for the nation of Israel, praying in a way that shows us the true need and humility demanded in a corporate prayer of repentance. Daniel was not personally guilty of most of what he confessed, but as a part of the nation he accepted personal responsibility. The Western highly individualized mind has a difficult time grasping this concept, but our nation and our churches would be much better off if we had a deeper communal way of thinking and acting. As the chapter continues, we are introduced to Gabriel, one of God's archangels. He flies in to visit Daniel in response to that amazing prayer.

In chapter 10, later historically, Daniel received a vision about a great war to come, and he was so smitten by it that he fasted and prayed for three weeks. The result of that extended prayer time was the appearance of another angel, most likely Gabriel as well, although he is not named. He told Daniel that his prayer had been heard three weeks earlier but that he had been detained in a battle with the prince of Persia, evidently an archangel of Satan. When Michael the archangel, called here "one of the chief princes," came to help in the battle, Gabriel was freed up to come in answer to the prayer of Daniel offered three weeks earlier.

The final time God pulled back this curtain to reveal the spiritual battle in its massive scope is described in Revelation 12. The first 11 chapters of Revelation showed the causes and results of the persecution of God's early Christians from an earthly perspective. You can read my book, *Revelation Revealed*,[19] for those details. Then in chapter 12, the Spirit takes us behind the scenes to the

---

19. Gordon Ferguson, *Revelation Revealed: The Keys to Unlocking the Mysteries of Revelation* (Spring, TX: Illumination Publishers, 2013).

spiritual realm of the battle, and then in the following chapters shows how that battle between God and Satan plays out until it is over, and God's final victory is won. Here is the passage that sets the stage.

Revelation 12:7–12

[7] Then war broke out in heaven. Michael and his angels fought against the dragon, and the dragon and his angels fought back. [8] But he was not strong enough, and they lost their place in heaven. [9] The great dragon was hurled down—that ancient serpent called the devil, or Satan, who leads the whole world astray. He was hurled to the earth, and his angels with him. [10] Then I heard a loud voice in heaven say: "Now have come the salvation and the power and the kingdom of our God, and the authority of his Messiah. For the accuser of our brothers and sisters, who accuses them before our God day and night, has been hurled down. [11] They triumphed over him by the blood of the Lamb and by the word of their testimony; they did not love their lives so much as to shrink from death. [12] Therefore rejoice, you heavens and you who dwell in them! But woe to the earth and the sea, because the devil has gone down to you! He is filled with fury, because he knows that his time is short."

A Bit of Conjecture

This monumental spiritual battle that Adam and Eve were created into and their ability to overcome would factor into one of the primary purposes of their creation. They were creatures of choice, the only such creatures in planet earth's adventure. The Bible doesn't say much about the origin of Satan, but logic would say that he and the angels were also creatures of choice. However, he made horrific choices with irreversible horrific consequences. He was the only creature to choose rebellion against God without external temptation. Once that rebellion occurred, he evidently recruited other angels to join him, and thus the galactic spiritual battle began.

Would it not seem obvious that humans were created to not only join in this battle, but to somehow demonstrate to the satanic world something that God knew had to be a part of ultimate world history—both the spiritual world and the physical world? Yes, that is conjecture on my part, but our battle with that satanic world taking place all day, every day, was not mere coincidence. It simply had to be a matter of divine design and purpose. Thankfully, being among the "few" on the narrow road that leads to life eternal with God puts us in a marvelous place within God's spiritual world. For example, when you are in a church assembly praising God, you see only a small part of the assembly, as Hebrews reveals.

Hebrews 12:22–24
[22] But you have come to Mount Zion, to the city of the living God, the heavenly Jerusalem. You have come to thousands upon thousands of angels in joyful assembly, [23] to the church of the firstborn, whose names are written in heaven. You have come to God, the Judge of all, to the spirits of the righteous made perfect, [24] to Jesus the mediator of a new covenant, and to the sprinkled blood that speaks a better word than the blood of Abel.

Whatever else may be biblically observed or logically conjectured, this much is true. The original pair of humans, in spite of their initial sin, still had a better shot at resisting Satan as a more complete *imago Dei* than separately. It was not good for the man to be alone, nor was it good for the woman to be alone. Ecclesiastes 4 was not wrong—two are better than one. That was true of Adam and Eve, and it is true of you and your mate if you are married. We would sin more, and more grievously, without the help of our mates. I am my wife's *'ezer* (the Hebrew for helper) and she is my *'ezer* in our spiritual battles individually and collectively. Even if we are single, God tells us we as his people never have to be alone. We have his Spirit within, and our spiritual family as well. The triune nature of God proclaims that as his image-bearers, we are made for communal relationships, for connection. I'm sure more is involved here in God's purposes for creating male and female as his *imago Dei*, but that's enough to get us thinking beyond the creation of Eve as a nice little helper for Adam, to be his sex partner, chief cook, and bottle washer. That is, in the bigger picture of things, quite a ludicrous assumption—by male egos run amok.

A Suitable Helper

Since it was not good for the man to be alone, needing a woman to give a more complete picture of the *imago Dei*, that missing part was called in Genesis 2:18, a "suitable helper." We miss the meaning of this term by a country mile as well, if we picture her as that nice little helper as described in the above paragraph. Let's address the original woman as being a suitable helper. What does that mean, and what do we normally think it means? The Hebrew word for suitable helper is *'ezer kenegdo,* literally a helper corresponding to the man as a suitable counterpart. *'Ezer* is used mostly in the Old Testament to show God as a helper of his people, often in military settings, interestingly.

Rolan Monje, one of the contributing authors to the book on gender issues written by members of our movement's teacher service team, and one of the most accomplished Hebrew scholars in our family of churches, wrote this in an email exchange in response to a quote I read about *'ezer* being used mainly in a setting of military help:

> It is interesting that the term is used regularly for God helping his people, including martial deliverance, so 'ezer does have a sense of being more than ordinary help in those instances...I think it's

safe to say that 'ezer denotes capacity and strength or might, and has military connotations in certain contexts. I also agree that together 'ezer kenegdo (two words) forms a powerful image, but I would say it speaks more to equality (being his "match" or "counterpart") and importance (being an "ally") rather than being a co-warrior. One could speak of the woman as being an "indispensable companion" or "help one cannot do without."[20]

Suffice it to say that the term is used repeatedly and most often of God himself being a helper. To weaken the concept of an 'ezer helper by suggesting any sort of inferiority being involved in its application to women is not only dead wrong; it's insulting to God (and to women).

Worse Theology Follows

As bad as the theology drawn from Genesis 2:18 often is, it pales in comparison to the bone-crunching historical misinterpretation of Genesis 3:16.

> **Genesis 3:16 (NASB)**
> To the woman He said, "I will greatly multiply Your pain in childbirth, In pain you will bring forth children; Yet your desire will be for your husband, and he will rule over you."

For centuries, this verse has been ripped out of its context and viewed as the intended will of God for husband and wife. She would desire and submit to her husband as he ruled over her. How nice, how sweet, how WRONG! Yet, we have so often missed that the context of the verse is clearly amid curses brought on by sin. Satan and the ground are cursed by God and humans bear the consequences. Men's lot in life would be made worse by having to raise food to sustain life in soil covered with thorns and thistles. Women

---

20. Email correspondence, March 16, 2023.

would have increased pain in childbirth and be ruled over by husbands. Not a nice picture for either gender. The words *desire* and *rule* in Hebrew are not necessarily suggestive of bad desires or bad ruling, but history played this out in a battle of the sexes in which one principle prevailed—"Might makes right!" What becomes clear is that Genesis 3:16 was *descriptive* of what sin would usher in, not *prescriptive* of what God ever wanted.

To be more precise, that principle of domination has a very definite name and definition—patriarchy. We easily assume that *patriarchy* is just applicable to the husband/wife relationship based on this verse, but that doesn't come close to describing the extremes that have ensued. Merriam-Webster defines patriarchy as "a social organization marked by the supremacy of the father in the clan or family, the legal dependence of wives and children, and the reckoning of descent and inheritance in the male line. broadly: control by men of a disproportionately large share of power."[21]

What is called "primogeniture" is a related concept found in the Old Testament and in human history, generally. It dictates that the eldest son (male) receives a disproportionate amount of family inheritance. Vocabulary.com notes: "It may seem vastly unfair, but primogeniture dates back to the Old Testament. Examples of this practice in which the first-born son receives exclusive inheritance rights can be found throughout history and around the world—from the Middle East to Medieval Europe." In most societies currently, its gentler manifestation can at least be seen through showing favoritism to the firstborn in many families, especially to the firstborn male. Like other forms of patriarchy, both males and females are hurt by it, often deeply.

Here is the point that we simply must see, because patriarchy invades humanity with consequences which are almost beyond comprehension. Carolyn James, in her book, *Malestrom* (one of my favorites), describes it as well as anyone.

---

21. https://www.merriam-webster.com/dictionary/patriarchy#:~:text=noun,inheritance%20in%20the%20male%20line

One of the often ignored but most destructive consequences of the malestrom is the fact that not all men are beneficiaries of the powers of patriarchy but are, ironically, among the greatest casualties... The fall and the curse that opened the door for men to rule over women ignited a dark ambition in the souls of men that extends a perverted sense of rule to their brothers. It began with Cain's violent murder of Abel and escalated into the creation of tribes and empires, widespread oppression, and endless wars. Genocide, ethnic cleansing, massacre, holocaust, apartheid, discrimination, slavery, caste and class, racism, profiling, abuse, and elitism these are just a short list of obscene concepts that inevitably take a terrible toll in the lives of men and boys. Expressions of male violence against other men have overrun the planet and dominate the news.[22]

Her book is introduced by a foreword written by her husband, Frank A. James III, President and Professor of Historical Theology at Biblical Theological Seminary. As I began to read the book, I did read the foreword first. My heart started pounding as I read it, and after finishing I wrote at the top of the page my initial reaction to the book's subject: "This foreword contains the most accurate, therefore the saddest, definition of the male gender that I have ever read." Here is a partial quote to help you understand why I wrote what I did.

I also know from my own life experiences that even as men pursue the various culturally defined visions of manhood, it is often accompanied by a gnawing sense within us (the *imago dei*) that there is something not quite right about our behaviors and attitudes—the constant jousting for superiority, the artificial machismo, the domineering bravado, the denigration of the weaker males, and the sexualizing of women that shapes so much of male conversation.

---

22. Carolyn Custis James, *Malestrom: Manhood Swept into the Currents of a Changing World* (Grand Rapids, MI: Zondervan, 2015), 134.

The truth is that the malestrom produces schizophrenic males. We present to the world one version of ourselves for external consumption. We hide the true self with its wounds and vulnerabilities. Sometimes we bury the authentic self so deeply that it surfaces only when lubricated by alcohol or drugs. This schizophrenic maleness proliferates in our homes, locker rooms, movie theaters, magazines, blogs, and to our shame, our pulpits, Sunday school classes, and campus ministries. And yes, it is alive and well in our evangelical seminaries.[23]

I think he was spot-on in describing males who have not been recreated in Christ, and the large majority of those who have been still have lingering vestiges of their insecurities inside them, mostly kept hidden. Male insecurities arise in those who aren't quite sure who they are, or they are not quite comfortable with who they think they are. I remember reading an article back in the mid-1980s in a major magazine about highly successful businesspeople (who were in the majority males). They were asked in a very confidential setting a certain very probing question. Confidentiality was assured by the promise that no names or otherwise identifying personal information would be used in the article based on the interviews.

The question posed went something like this: "As a highly successful businessperson, what is your greatest fear?" By far the most common answer was that they lived in fear that their superiors and fellow workers would discover who they *really* were. In other words, the person they saw in the mirror every day was in their minds different (and quite inferior) to the one other people thought they were. They felt as though they were projecting a façade which was almost the opposite of how they felt about themselves, and thus they lived in fear of being exposed. Why did they, and why do we, employ such acting in putting on a false front,

---

23. James, *Malestrom*, 9.

trying to convince others that we are not who we feel like we really are? In a word, Patriarchy.

Males Lead the Parade

The realities of Genesis 3:16 have been a constant reminder of what humanity is capable of, and males have always led the parade from then until now. Who can deny it? Surely no one when you consider the shocking statistics, manly statistics at that. Human history has endured a total number killed in wars estimated as high as 1 billion. The School of Public Policy at the University of Maryland states this in their online presence: "An itemized total sum of deaths in wars and conflicts 'killed or allowed to die by human decision' of approximately 231 million for the 100 years of the 20th Century."[24]

These figures reflect the realities; we are going in the worst direction possible, even with the amazing advances in human knowledge and technology. The ever-increasing devastating effects of patriarchy have pushed mankind (malekind, to invent another word) to the brink of annihilation. One push of a button, sending out hundreds of missiles with nuclear warheads is all that stands in the way.

The Real Genesis of This Article

I first taught much of this material in a lesson for the 2023 "Western Elders' Retreat" in Denver on the topic of elders and evangelists working together. Church leadership has always been infiltrated with patriarchy and it is almost impossible to eradicate it. The inner, perhaps unrecognized, desire for recognition continues to ignite our efforts to gain power and control. The best of us is not immune to its insidious grasp. Following a pattern principle, I think it is assumed that since patriarchy is so practiced in the Bible

---

24. "Deaths in Wars and Conflicts in the 20th Century," School of Public Policy: Center for International & Security Studies at Maryland, June 20, 2006, https://cissm.umd.edu/research-impact/publications/deaths-wars-and-conflicts-20th-century.

that it must be God's plan. Really? Polygamy? Violence? Misogyny? It is so deeply entrenched. We can read Matthew 20 about the greatest leaders being servants and the greatest of all leaders being a slave, but few seem able to understand what is being said and still fewer put it into practice. All our guesses about Satan's favorite tool to capture us are missing the point if we do not see that one of his favorite tools is to keep the fires of patriarchy burning ever brighter and hotter. We have been a world at war since the beginning, for sure since Genesis 3:16.

I ended that lesson with three quotations, the first two sent to me by Tom Jones and the third my own. Here they are:

- Power is not controlling other people. Power is controlling yourself. Trying to control other people is the first sign that you are entirely out of control. Controlling others is what weak people think power looks like. (Kalen Dion, poet)

- If humility is the key to the kingdom and no one enters it without humility, patriarchy, which is more associated with pride and control, may bring to mind another camel that cannot go through the eye of a needle. (Tom Jones)

- Team leadership cannot be successful long term unless we truly embrace what Jesus taught in Matthew 20 and refuse to fit into the world's views of leadership. I personally think that these issues cannot be fixed without fixing what I believe is a distorted, unbiblical view of women, in both our physical and spiritual families. (Gordon Ferguson)

To be forthright with you, I have been amazed and puzzled at how deeply embedded in our church movement's psyche is the idea of authority and control and how we can repeatedly read Matthew 20 yet return to early worldly views of authority. It feels staggering to me. May God help us get the world's DNA out of our hardwired brains, brains which are thus miswired. I believe that the problem cannot be solved without an uprooting of patriarchy among us, which necessarily means that our view of women in the church must return to God's original plan of mutuality expressed in Genesis 1 and 2. This change requires both reflection and repentance concerning ways we can uproot these from our personal and collective minds and practices. But there is more, as we move to the New Testament.

Chapter 4

A New Testament Perspective:
Part 1: Great Expecations Aroused!

My original intent in starting this writing was to confine myself to covering two parts within one or two articles for my website: a historical perspective (Part 1) and a biblical perspective (Part 2). While neither of those parts was expected to be short, it became obvious as I wrote that at least four parts were likely needed. The last three planned were to fall under the heading of "a biblical perspective." This perspective was to include an Old Testament perspective, a New Testament perspective, and a broader, general Bible perspective sharing stories and insights about specific women in the Bible, from both Old and New Testaments.

It also became obvious that another part would be needed to show in more detail the hermeneutical errors ushered in by pattern, or blueprint theology, which is a part of Restoration Movement DNA, including our segment of the RM. We have had some rather strange practices that deserve a closer look as a natural outgrowth of trying to effectively deal with the overall topic. One more aspect of this topic, spiritual formation, which will never be complete without the female addition into male development, led to yet another chapter. Eventually, I ended up with a book of nine chapters, with the NT perspective expanded into three chapters.

Acts 2: Shocks to the System!

Acts 2 contains some jolting surprises to first century Jews who were gathered in Jerusalem to celebrate the Day of Pentecost.

The fulfillment of Joel 2:28–32 had finally arrived, and it did so with a bang—quite early in the morning at that. This was a new type of wakeup call, no doubt. The outpouring of the Holy Spirit was a shock in two ways, the actual event and the promises thus enabled by the Spirit's coming. The sights and sounds must have been spectacular, for they attracted a crowd of thousands very quickly. The apostles were speaking in many different languages and the crowd, comprised of visitors from 17 nations, understood at least the part of what they heard in their own languages. They understood enough to be amazed and to search for the meaning of it all. The easy explanation was that the apostles were drunk, but Peter soon debunked that story by reminding them that it was only 9am. Then he quoted the passage being fulfilled.

Acts 2:17–21

[17] "In the last days, God says, I will pour out my Spirit on all people. Your sons and daughters will prophesy, your young men will see visions, your old men will dream dreams. [18] Even on my servants, both men and women, I will pour out my Spirit in those days, and they will prophesy. [19] I will show wonders in the heavens above and signs on the earth below, blood and fire and billows of smoke. [20] The sun will be turned to darkness and the moon to blood before the coming of the great and glorious day of the Lord. [21] And everyone who calls on the name of the Lord will be saved."

The promises that were based on this outpouring were also a shock to the system of Judaism, based on their knowledge of the Old Testament. In it, only special people received the Holy Spirit, but now everyone could be a recipient of that outpouring. Peter clarified how this could occur later in the chapter, saying that every repentant person baptized would receive the Spirit as an indwelling guest (verse 38). Wow! How exciting that must have been to hear. This promised New Covenant was new indeed. Forgiveness of sins, along with the Holy Spirit, would be given when baptized, corresponding to calling on the name of the Lord and being saved in Joel 2:32. (See also Acts 22:16 for a similar description.)

Surely one of the biggest shocks was the obvious exalting of the role of women. Some of the rabbinical quotes of that time showed how little women were valued. One supposed popular men's prayer included thanking God that they were born neither a Gentile nor a woman.[25] Jewish women had their own court in the temple area, but they were absolutely forbidden to enter the men's court. Joel's prophecy was nothing, if not radical, in this regard. Sons and daughters would prophesy; God's servants, both men and women, would prophesy. The promise of the indwelling Spirit for all as a seal of Divine ownership and sonship was one thing, but having the Spirit poured out on those to receive the gift of prophecy was quite another. Just imagine—women inspired by the Holy Spirit to speak for God, to speak his words to the people!

With this awesome inauguration of the New Covenant came many unexpected sights, sounds, and promises. But one of the biggest surprises must have been to the females in the audience. Jesus' breaking of accepted interactions between men and woman had been no accident. He was preparing the way for a radical kingdom relationship between his spiritual sons and daughters, longed for by women and perhaps dreaded by some (most?) men. But the tide was set to change with the events of Pentecost, and change it did.

Jesus said that heaven would not be about gender, since we would be as the angels. Teaching his followers to pray, "Your kingdom come. Your will be done, on earth as it is in heaven," meant more than we might imagine. Be careful what you pray for, the old saying goes. If you are still in the clutches of patriarchy, you might best leave out that part of the Lord's prayer. Surprises in the now/ not yet phases of the kingdom had arrived, although they were

---

25. "My Jewish Learning," https://www.myjewishlearning.com/article/who-has-not-made-me-a-woman/.

likely not understood initially any better than the inclusion of the Gentiles was understood. But God would make it all clear as his kingdom spread. How clear is it to us even now?

God's Kingdom of Heaven on Earth—Now and Not Yet

One of the challenges facing us is in our understanding of the concept of God's plan for the kingdom in its present earthly phase and how much of the future phase it should encompass here and now. One possible clue is found in how the kingdom is designated by the New Testament writers. All except Matthew call it the kingdom of God, or something very close to that. Matthew almost exclusively calls it the kingdom of heaven. That is striking, and surely not by accident. His Gospel had the most Jewish flavor of the Gospel accounts, which suggests that he focused on what Jesus prayed in the "model prayer" of Matthew 6, especially verse 10 as quoted in the preceding paragraph. I think it likely that Jesus in that prayer had in mind Genesis 1 and 2, prior to sin's destructive entrance into the world.

As we have already described it in Chapter 3, an often overlooked yet highly significant aspect of God's creation of both male and female was to reflect his image more fully, the *imago Dei*. Bringing the concept into the New Testament, how would his image best be reflected? In Jesus, for sure.

Colossians 1:19
[19] For it was the *Father's* good pleasure for all the fullness to dwell in Him,

Colossians 2:9
[9] For in Him all the fullness of Deity dwells in bodily form,

Hebrews 1:3a
[3] And He is the radiance of His glory and the exact representation of His nature...

However, very similar terms are used to describe the universal church, the kingdom of heaven on earth. In the second of these, it might seem to be saying that we as individuals could become the fullness of God, but "you" is plural here, thus also referring to the church. Ephesians 4:13 is preceded by a specific reference to the body, or church.

Ephesians 1:22–23
[22] And He put all things in subjection under His feet, and gave Him as head over all things to the church, [23] which is His body, the fullness of Him who fills all in all.

Ephesians 3:19
[19] and to know the love of Christ which surpasses knowledge, that you may be filled up to all the fullness of God.

Ephesians 4:13
[13] until we all attain to the unity of the faith, and of the knowledge of the Son of God, to a mature man, to the measure of the stature which belongs to the fullness of Christ.

Just as Jesus was the manifestation of God, the kingdom of heaven on earth as the church is the manifestation of Christ. God could not be grasped to the greatest extent possible by humans until he was seen in flesh and blood, and by the same token, Christ could not be grasped to the greatest extent possible by humans until he was (and is) seen in flesh and blood (us). And thus, the kingdom of heaven is presented as the ultimate *imago Dei* for the final age of planet earth until the return of Jesus.

It should be noted that the word church (from the Greek *ekklesia*) has come to mean something very different than originally intended. Even the idea of assembly is different from what the root word meaning would have originally intended. Most people think of church as something you attend primarily to have an experience with God, a vertical experience, without much emphasis on the horizontal experience of Christian fellowship. Worse, church is a reference to a building where people meet. The best idea to convey church is simply God's family. The actual intent is something like community, a spiritual community whose lives are intertwined with God and one another. Nothing less could convey the *imago Dei* effectively.

Given the highly significant ramifications of these theological facts, who can doubt that the goal of Jesus was to see his kingdom on earth come as close as possible to the ultimate kingdom in heaven? For this reason, God was always striking blows against the disastrous consequences of patriarchy and primogeniture throughout human history. As we will see in Chapter 7, he did it time and time again in the Old Testament, but multiplied the attack through the ministry of Christ and in the new covenant. One of the most obvious ways Jesus did this was in how he viewed, related to, and highlighted women in his earthly sojourn. He was working to restore as much of the original *imago Dei* as possible, even in the midst of the world's demonstration of patriarchy and its effects.

God's Kingdom in Assembly

With that in mind, how could the assembled church not be a highly significant part of this goal? Disciples today are always anxious to have their friends and family attend church assemblies with them because of this precise point. Nothing will impact others more than seeing collective worship of God's people, with our special relational fellowship before and after the public worship period. God's image should be evident in any one of us, but the collective impact of God's kingdom in assembled worship provides the most compelling evidence possible. We might consider that this setting should present the purest form of what life on earth was meant to be before sin blocked the light of that original creation.

Interestingly, N.T. Wright, considered by many to be the greatest living New Testament scholar, took this very approach in giving an exposition of 1 Corinthians 11.

> The underlying point then seems to be that in worship it is important for both men and women to be their truly created selves, to honour God by being what they are and not blurring the lines by pretending to be something else. One of the unspoken clues to this passage may be Paul's assumption that in worship the creation is being restored, or perhaps that in worship we are anticipating its eventual restoration (15.27–28). God made humans male and female, and gave them 'authority' over the world, as Ben-Sirach 17.3 puts it, summarizing Genesis 1.26–28 and echoing Psalm 8.4–8 (Ben-Sirach was written around 200 BC). And if humans are to reclaim this authority over the world, this will come about as they worship the true God, as they pray and prophesy in his name, and are renewed in his image, in being what they were made to be, in celebrating the genders God has given them.[26]

Let's Get Really Practical

How much impact would our services have if we still had slaves and slave owners as a part of it? How much impact would our services have if we had obvious caste and racial distinctions among us? Actually, we do have a fairly obvious caste system in at least one sense, that condemned the showing of favoritism toward the rich (James 2). We must be careful to not repeat that sin in our materialistic admiration of the highly successful and highly endowed financially.

For example, I've observed through many decades in different churches that the elder with the most influence is the one having the greatest worldly success and the money that goes with it.

---

26. N.T. Wright, "Women's Service in the Church: The Biblical Basis," a conference paper for the Symposium, 'Men, Women and the Church' St John's College, Durham, September 4, 2004.

"Head" elders may not be biblical, but they exist and are not hard to spot in far too many elderships I've observed through my decades in many churches. That said, too many members just accept the situation, perhaps even admire it. Shame on us! Galatians 3:28 says that such distinctions are to be done away with in Christ.

The first century assemblies described in 1 Corinthians 11 saw both men and women praying and prophesying, with the only distinction which was dictated by local culture. Paul had already made it quite clear two chapters earlier that becoming all things to all people to save as many as possible was of paramount importance. The image of God should be seen in every way possible, in every place possible, and the best place possible was when the kingdom of God assembled to worship as his kingdom on earth. Are God's purposes for males and females in his original creation and now in his new creation different? Surely, only patriarchy could answer in the affirmative. I certainly cannot.

Did that Early Church Have Female Prophets?

Based on the promises of Joel 2, of course they did. Philip, a well-known figure in the early church, having been chosen by the Spirit as one of the Seven (Acts 6) and as the one to plant the first church in Samaria (Acts 8), must have been so proud to have been the father of four daughters with the gift of prophecy (Acts 21:9). I would have loved to have been a fly on the wall listening to the theological discussions and sharing of experiences that took place in that house! In the Old Testament times, fathers would have bragged only about the exploits of their sons, with an occasional mention of their daughters when they bore them grandchildren. But now a new day had dawned and a father like Philip would have heard compliments and praise for his prophesying daughters. God had been chipping away at patriarchy and its kissing cousin, primogeniture, all through the Old Testament, but now he was pulling out his sledgehammer to begin demolition.

When we read 1 Corinthians 11, we see that women were

doing what Joel 2 and Acts 2 said that they would do—prophesy. There were cultural issues that Paul said should be followed, but there is no doubt that women prophesied. Also, there seems to be little doubt that this context is one of a public service, in fact a Sunday service. At this point, those who are disturbed by women speaking in a public setting with men and women both in the audience begin to put the focus on any type of female limitation they can find or invent and rely on "patterns" to do so. Patriarchy is for some men like a disease that cannot be cured—it first invades their emotions and from there spreads to the intellect. From that point, some really strange things enter the discussion, as may be seen in the following comments from what I call the "Complementarian Bible," *Recovering Biblical Manhood and Womanhood*, edited by John Piper and Wayne Grudem.

> Prophecy in the worship of the early church was not the kind of authoritative, infallible revelation we associate with the written prophecies of the Old Testament. It was a report in human words based on a spontaneous, personal revelation from the Holy Spirit (1 Corinthians 14:30) for the purpose of edification, encouragement, consolation, conviction, and guidance (1 Corinthians 14:3, 24–25; Acts 21:4; 16:6–10). It was not necessarily free from a mixture of human error, and thus needed assessment (1 Thessalonians 5:19–20; 1 Corinthians 14:29) on the basis of the apostolic (Biblical) teaching (1 Corinthians 14:36–38; 2 Thessalonians 2:1–3). Prophecy in the early church did not correspond to the sermon today or to a formal exposition of Scripture. Both women and men could stand and share what they believed God had brought to mind for the good of the church.[27]

You may rest assured that these men were not taught such an indefinite view of prophecy in their first course in Seminary

---

27. John Piper and Wayne Grudem, *Recovering Biblical Manhood and Womanhood: A Response to Evangelical Feminism* (Wheaton, IL: Crossway, 1991), 70.

addressing the nature of the Bible. I remember that course and later taught it many times myself in a ministry training school. Until you begin talking about prophecy delivered by females, prophecy has always been described as an inspired message from God to humans through the Holy Spirit. You will also want to conduct a closer examination of the passages used in their quote for their proof and how many manipulative assumptions regarding those texts are made. Conservative commentators on those texts will aptly point out that the examination of prophecy was to spot a false prophet, not false content by a divinely inspired prophet, male or female. In all my study throughout a long ministry career, I have never encountered statements about prophecy remotely resembling those made in this book by Piper and Grudem. You must make up definitions when the biblical passages don't support deeply embedded hierarchical views.

Look at a concordance and see how the term prophecy is used repeatedly in the Bible. In Deuteronomy 18, after Moses promised that an ultimate prophet would come to them, speaking of Jesus, we find this explanation of true and false prophets.

Deuteronomy 18:20–22
But a prophet who presumes to speak in my name anything I have not commanded, or a prophet who speaks in the name of other gods, is to be put to death." [21] You may say to yourselves, "How can we know when a message has not been spoken by the LORD?" [22] If what a prophet proclaims in the name of the LORD does not take place or come true, that is a message the LORD has not spoken. That prophet has spoken presumptuously, so do not be alarmed.

Speaking of written Scripture, Peter had this to say in 2 Peter 1:20–21:

Above all, you must understand that no prophecy of Scripture came about by the prophet's own interpretation of things. [21] For prophecy never had its origin in the human will, but prophets, though human, spoke from God as they were carried along by the Holy Spirit.

This passage makes it clear that prophesying places the Holy Spirit in charge of delivering the message from God through the prophet. The mystery of Christ, once hidden but now revealed, came from God's Spirit through the apostles and prophets (Ephesians 3:5). The church in Antioch, responsible for sending out Paul on his missionary journeys, was led by prophets and teachers, with no mention of either elders or evangelists. Those with the gift of prophecy had a dominant role in the early church and its mission. In the lists of leaders given to the church in Ephesians 4:11, the order is apostles and then prophets, mentioned before evangelists and elders.

In a similar passage listing miraculous gifts (1 Corinthians 12:28), Paul was even more specific. "And God has placed in the church first of all apostles, second prophets, third teachers, then miracles, then gifts of healing, of helping, of guidance, and of different kinds of tongues." And yet Grudem and Piper describe women prophesying in terms that I doubt they ever used of prophecy until they felt compelled to admit that women did in fact prophesy, just as Peter promised through quoting Joel 2 in Acts 2. Can we not just let the great expectations aroused by Joel 2 and Acts 2 excite us and lead us forward, rather than look for ways to explain them away?

Chapter 5

A New Testament Perspective:
Part 2: Where is the Best Starting Place?

Since the kingdom of God showed up in dramatic ways at Pentecost, it would seem this would be an appropriate starting place to view a New Testament perspective concerning women in the church. The Christian church, described as the family of God, formed as believers were added to the church family by the Spirit of God. In the account of this powerful beginning of a new way in Acts 2, we are reminded of prophecies in Joel 2, as noted in the previous chapter. Though we read of women prophesying in the new covenant, two verses in the Epistles are often interpreted by complementarians (born of patriarchy) as contradicting these prophecies and the events described in 1 Corinthians 11:5. To gain background in interpreting these verses, I believe the concept of family is an important consideration.

Families are of God. With the creation of the original pair, the first family began. Later, a broader spiritual family was begun and can be found in different phases throughout the Bible. After the creation of the first family God used a person (Abraham), then a community (Israel), and then the church to portray and create spiritual family. When the new covenant arrives, God's spiritual family is the church community. Since both types of families are creations of God, we should expect many of the same principles to apply to both. Although my original intent was to simply address 1 Corinthians 14:34–35 and 1 Timothy 2:12 and their contexts, I believe it important to view Ephesians 5 as Paul refers to the family.

This scripture addresses various family-related relationships, and its context provides the ideal starting place for a closer look at family.

We note that the NIV 2011 version places Ephesians 5:21–6:9 under the heading of "Instructions for Christian Households." The instructions could also appropriately be called "Family Codes," which were common in the Roman Empire of that day. However, those societal codes were not Christian codes. Given the deeply entrenched principles of patriarchy and primogeniture, you don't need to have much imagination to guess how the roles of slaves, children (especially female), and wives were described and regulated. The "man of the house" in such codes was decidedly the dominant force and ultimate ruler of his domain.

Paul's Christian version of family codes would have been viewed as remarkable in that first century setting. Of all things, he addressed how slave owners should view and treat their slaves, those who were ordinarily seen as property, like animals. According to 6:9, they were to treat their slaves in the same way that slaves were to serve their masters—wholeheartedly as if they were serving the Lord and to never threaten them. Such teaching was unheard of in that day outside the family of God. Slaves were to obey masters with fear, respect, and sincerity of heart just as they would obey Christ (6:5–8). This reciprocity of treatment would have been not only unusual to the average Roman citizen, but quite shocking.

I begin with a view of the household codes to prepare us for the radical differences in the whole list. As we continue to work our way backwards, we next encounter the household codes between parents and children. In 6:4, fathers are instructed to avoid exasperating their children, and instead to train and instruct them in the Lord's ways. Shocking once again! Mothers were seen as primarily responsible for raising children, but Paul instructs Christian fathers to not only to train their children, but to train them regardless of gender, thus putting female children on equal footing with the male children. We have difficulty recognizing how countercultural these Christian family codes were. In 6:1–3, the commands to obey parents and honor them were not new to Jewish ears, of course, but the contents of Ephesians 6:1–9 was radical compared to common household codes of the day.

Wives and Husbands

Paul begins his family codes in an unusual way, with a verse that sets the stage for the entire list. "Submit to one another out of reverence for Christ" (Ephesians 5:21). He states a needs-based servanthood principle for everyone he addresses in these codes. He writes not only of husbands and wives, but all of the relationships described in the list. He turns the conventional thinking about them upside down. We've already seen this in the slave/master, child/parent relationships. Slaves serve masters, but masters also serve slaves. Is that a surprise to you, given what Jesus said in Matthew 20 and parallel passages about spiritual leadership? Applying that principle to slavery, the greatest slave owner was the greatest slave to his slave. Wow!

Jesus repeatedly said that to be a great leader, one should be a servant, and to be the greatest of all, one must be a slave of all. The principle of self-denial and considering the needs of others above one's own finds its way into NT teaching over and over. Jesus demonstrated that principle; Jesus, showing us God in flesh, was that principle. If the greatest of all is the slave of all, then Deity is not simply King of kings and Lord of lords, but most definitely Servant of servants.

As I stated in my video podcast series, *Eternity's Brink,* on my YouTube channel (Gordon Ferguson Teaching Ministry),[28] Jesus did not become a servant when he became a man. He became a man precisely because he was a servant. That thought came to me quite suddenly in the middle of the night amid a near death experience during a 23-day hospital stay. I had once heard this thought of Jesus becoming a man because he was a servant from my old friend, Jim McGuiggan, but as I was contemplating the real possibility of meeting God at any moment, it popped back into my

---

28. https://www.youtube.com/channel/UCIBbIlxgkMfvAm084RtpqSw.

mind. If we can grasp the principle, it will forever change our view of authority in the family of God in every possible relationship. It undoubtedly permeates this list of household codes in Ephesians.

Children serve parents through obedience and honoring them. Parents, and fathers in particular, serve children by loving them, treating them respectfully, and training them to love and serve God. These household codes from start to finish are designed to teach the very heart of what following Jesus is all about—servanthood. Using any part of this passage to emphasize authority and control borders on the edge of blasphemy, a term defined as "the act or offense of speaking sacrilegiously about God or sacred things."[29] We are discussing the things of God, sacred things. Yet, the mentality of patriarchy has led many Christian oriented males (and females) to nearly the same conclusions regarding the husband/wife relationship that the average Roman held in the first century. The husband is the boss of the household, including his wife, and she had better submit to him as the leader or be guilty of sin before God.

Since this passage in Ephesians 5 is about self-denial and serving and meeting needs, how do we come to focus on authority, position, and power? Is it not patriarchy? Remember *Merriam-Webster's* definition of patriarchy: "social organization marked by the supremacy of the father in the clan or family, the legal dependence of wives and children, and the reckoning of descent and inheritance in the male line. broadly: control by men of a disproportionately large share of power." And hasn't that been a wonderful blessing to the world? Please excuse my sarcasm. I'm just broken-hearted about how Satan finds ways to deceive us, even when our intentions are good. Household codes in the Roman society of that day were all about authority and control by males; household codes in Ephesians were nothing about either, but rather about servant-hood and submission of everyone mentioned.

---

29. https://www.oxfordreference.com/display/10.1093/acref/9780198609810.001.0001/acref-9780198609810-e-897#:~:text=the%20action%20or%20offence%20of,Greek%20...%20...

The Main Focus is Not About Marriage Anyway!

Paul gave details about household relationships, so of course included the husband/wife relationship. The lessons therein are both practical and theological. But most who study the passage, including theologians, seem almost oblivious to Ephesians 5:32: "This is a profound mystery—but I am talking about Christ and the church." We miss the main focus of the entire context. The following is a very insightful excerpt from Michael Burns' doctoral dissertation research on the Corinthian correspondence, in which he also covers the Ephesians passage.

> The household code was used in Greek and Roman writing as a tool to describe the ideal ethic for a community. The household was viewed as the smallest political/economic unit, so it was easy to convey the cultural values through the smallest entity. The Romans especially wanted to display the genius and superiority of Roman hierarchy and order, so the codes demonstrated what kind of people they were to be. They keyed in on three key relationships. The husband-and-wife relationship was to be ordered as a socially elite person (husband) dealing with the socially inferior (wife). The parenting relationship was to be ordered as monarch and subject. The slave and master relationship was treated as owner and property.[30]

Paul blows that up by asserting that the church is to be a new kind of people. What kind of people? They are to be the submitting-to-one-another kind in every relationship. He subverts the Roman system by addressing the socially inferior, something not done in the normal household codes. This gave them all agency. It treated them as equal humans; an image-bearer. And so, when Paul says that wives should submit to their husbands, he is addressing them as equals and giving them the agency to choose to be a submitting-to-one-another kind of person. Not because they

---

30. From a conversation with Michael Burns, stemming from his doctoral dissertation research on Ephesians.

are required, but because they have the freedom to submit to their husband as they would to Christ.

He deepens the subversion by assigning responsibility in each case to the social superior (whereas the Roman codes only ever described the rights of the *pater familias,* or the male heads of the households). Paul is not explicitly teaching about marriage, although there are certainly implications for it. He is following the normal usage of the household code to demonstrate the values of the church and show what kind of community they are going to be. He even stresses this by clearly stating, "I'm talking here about Christ and the church" (verse 32).

Let the Women Speak for Themselves

One oddity that has accompanied the study of the women's role in the home and in the church is that until recently, it was addressed by male authors. That is parallel to having White males be the sole teachers about racial issues. The very fact that some of the best authors on the topic are women says a lot about why they were chosen as prophets in the early church and are more than capable of excellent teaching today—both in oral and written modes. Michelle Lee-Barnewall stated the principle of equality and inclusion quite well:

> When one can sufficiently bracket modern causes and read the text carefully in its original contexts, one sees that unity and inclusion prove more central than equality or freedom. A concern for love and humility, rather than one of authority and privilege, pervades the scriptural texts and contexts. If it should turn out that there are any roles reserved for men, this is in no way to give them unique privileges but rather to require distinctive responsibilities. What a contrast with the standard complementarian preoccupation with headship as leadership![31]

---

31. Michelle Lee-Barnewall, *Neither Complementarian nor Egalitarian: A Kingdom Corrective to the Evangelical Gender Debate* (Ada, MI: Baker Academic, 2016), from the foreword by Craig L. Blomberg.

Another female writer commended Lee-Barnewall's book, but said that she didn't go far enough. I tend to agree with that assessment:

> Notably absent is an attempt to address directly the damage caused by the sin of sexism. The changing views of women in the church aren't only due to mimicking cultural and secular "progress." They also represent, at least in part, a move towards repenting of denigration and abuse of women. As Christians, we must acknowledge that for much of the church's history, women were considered not only different, but actually inferior.
>
> It's not that, after calling for a change in conversation, I want to slip back into merely discussing questions of equality and authority. But once these questions are raised by history, we can't, as a church, simply change the subject. New ways of speaking about gender roles are deeply needed, but they cannot ignore context, history, and pain and abuse borne by women. Faithful and nuanced conversations about gender roles have to explicitly address the irrational ways we've been conditioned to regard women as inferior, unworthy, or less human than men.[32]

In recent years, I have felt increasingly compelled to write about both racial issues and women's issues for the same reason. Injustice is so consistently condemned in the Bible that Bible believers should feel righteous revulsion in their souls when they see those injustices in real life. Black people and females have been subject to some of the worst injustices in our American society, and history is strewn with nearly innumerable examples of injustices of many types. When anyone is made to feel inferior because of the color of their skin or because of their gender, something is badly wrong and terribly unrighteous.

---

32. Tish Harrison Warren, "Come Out of Your Gender-Role Foxholes," *Christianity Today*, July 1, 2016, https://www.christianitytoday.com/ct/2016/july-web-only/come-out-of-your-gender-role-foxholes.html.

As a White heterosexual male living amid societal injustices, experiencing them personally has not been my lot in life. But, as I have tried to understand what others who don't enjoy my privileges face and feel, I feel compelled to address it. I sometimes am tempted to leave it alone, to be honest. It isn't my own experience, after all. But God's Spirit won't let me drop it. Once I began delving into those two areas of systemic injustice, it became something like a compulsion. You can blame my compulsion all on me if you like, but I am going to blame a significant part of it on God. I've no doubt that he wants it addressed. In his Word, he uses the term justice well over 100 times. "But let justice roll on like a river, righteousness like a never-failing stream" (Amos 5:24).

You may be thinking, "Gordon, you are appealing too much to the emotions, not just letting the facts speak for themselves!" I appeal to facts and emotions. We are emotional beings. And have you not realized just how often Jesus and the writers of the Bible appealed to emotions? The Bible was not written like a master's thesis or a doctoral dissertation. Why would I want to write only in academic terms about issues that have taken a terrible toll on the emotions of our sisters in Christ, our own mothers and wives and sisters and daughters? No apologies coming from me on that front—none.

Is the Principle of Patriarchy Permanent in Marriage?

The New Testament was written when patriarchy was totally dominant. This accounts for so much of how the Bible was written. God in the flesh was male, although God is neither male nor female. God in the Bible is assigned the masculine pronoun. All of the twelve apostles initially chosen were male. It could not have been otherwise in that setting. We could say the same about the regulations given for slavery and polygamy, regulated yet not forbidden. These were undoubtedly intended by God to be ended by Christian principles in time.

In heaven, we humans will not be husbands or wives, said

Jesus (Matthew 22:30). Since we are to pray, "your kingdom come, your will be done, on earth as it is in heaven" (Matthew 6:10), how much of our earthly distinctions should be adhered to as absolutely permanent? Ephesians 2:6 says, "And God raised us up with Christ and seated us with him in the heavenly realms in Christ Jesus." This refers to the present. How much of heaven on earth are we prepared to embrace now, especially when we consider Galatians 3:28: "There is neither Jew nor Gentile, neither slave nor free, nor is there male and female, for you are all one in Christ Jesus?"

A Most Pivotal Verse—Galatians 3:28

In this section, I want to address some thoughts in a book written by members of the ICOC Teacher Service Team, *The Bible and Gender*.[33] I was a charter member of this group of dedicated teachers, served as its chairman for a time, am considered an "emeritus" member by the group, and was the grateful recipient of their first annual award, "Teacher of Teachers" in 2022. Most of the present members remain close friends of mine. Because the book is likely the most influential in my own family of churches, I feel the need to focus my comments in discussing Galatians 3:28 as it correlates with the book by my colleagues. While I could reference other chapters in that book, I wish to pose an important question relating to a stated conclusion concerning Galatians 3:28.

Chapter 4 opens with the statement: "Galatians 3:26–29 is one of the passages often cited in the context of gender discussions in the church."[34] The chapter is very well-written, and I agree with most of its conclusions except the one interpreting verse 28 more narrowly than I do, limiting the roles of women in ways I no longer see as limited. The chapter provides many excellent exegetical explanations and insights in a systematic, logical manner. Most of these insights would also be very helpful for those who have been

---

33. ICOC Teachers Service Team, *The Bible and Gender*, (Spring, TX: Illumination Publishers, 2020).

34. ICOC Teachers, *The Bible and Gender*, 61.

bitten with the "bug" of Torah pursuance (those who believe we are still to follow the Jewish laws). Overall, the complementarian view of this passage is presented about as well as I have seen it presented. (See Chapter 10 in *Discovering Biblical Equality* for an excellent exegesis of the same passage from an egalitarian viewpoint.)[35]

The chapter in *The Bible and Gender* argues that the primary goal of the letter is to show that the equality in verse 28 is simply a common salvation in Christ and all that it implies. The main issue I have with its primary conclusion about women in verse 28 is that it only deals with the obvious surface problems concerning salvation that affect the unity of those churches (and many others outside Galatia as well, as Romans would illustrate) without exploring surrounding issues. Beneath those presenting problems concerning salvation for all, serious ones to be sure, lies the question of why those problems are so serious. Romans 14 teaches, in essence, that it is permissible to agree to disagree without becoming disagreeable on some spiritual issues. Paul left no doubts that the main issue in Galatians does not fall within the realm of such "disputable" matters. But why not?

The unity which has been broken by the false teaching of the Judaizers must be restored by correcting this teaching of salvation availability for all. To be precise, the author sees this not as simply the main goal of the passage, but the only goal. "Paul is focused on the problem of false teaching in the Galatian churches. There is no other purpose."[36] This sentence seems to me to go well beyond any human's ability to judge fully the purposes of God in anything he does.

My question is prompted by the generally accepted concept that New Testament Scriptures often carry both a surface level meaning and a deeper level meaning, and I believe that verse 28 here is one such example. Unity ideally must provide the *imago*

---

35. Ronald W. Pierce, Rebecca Merrill Groothuis, and Gordon D. Fee, *Discovering Biblical Equality: Complementarity Without Hierarchy* (Westmont, IL: IVP Academic, 2021), 172–185, Kindle.

36. ICOC Teachers, *The Bible and Gender*, 75.

Dei as fully as possible, and to accomplish that, relationships must reflect humanity before sin entered the world. God's image cannot be reflected fully where oppression (power over others), division, or hierarchy (superior status levels) exist. These comments by Hicks support this idea very pointedly.

> The language of Galatians 3:28 is drawn from the creation account (Genesis 1:27). Paul uses "male and female" rather than "man or woman." This is not typical for Paul who only uses "female" elsewhere in Romans 1:26–27. He draws the language directly from Genesis. Paul echoes the original vision of creation where "male and female" form an explicit partnership and share responsibility for the creation. This creation language is driven by the hope of new creation in the "present evil age" (Galatians 1:4).[37]

From a practical vantage point, how is the unity of Galatians 3:28 even possible without equality? Can a Jew and a Gentile ever be completely unified without equality, in answer to this prayer request by Jesus? "Your kingdom come on earth as it is in heaven." Can a slave and a free person ever experience complete unity without equality? Can a male and a female?

Suppose we grant that equality exists in all areas pertaining to full salvation for all six categories of people mentioned in the verse. Thus, we are one in Christ, all standing on level ground at the foot of the cross, each being equally saved by the blood of Christ. But now suppose that only those with Jewish backgrounds are chosen for leadership roles (a blatant contradiction to the very opposite in Acts 6 when all seven deacons chosen are Greeks). Suppose that only free persons, non-slaves, are appointed to leadership roles. How do you think that would have worked in the first century or would go over in the twenty-first century?

And yet, we are being asked to accept this very reality when

---

37. Hicks, *Women Serving*, 115, Kindle.

applied to male and female. I think this happens for two basic reasons. One, we have failed to interpret two of Paul's other texts in their historical, cultural context. Two, we have failed to recognize and practice the fact that spiritual gifts, including those of teaching and leadership in Romans 12:6–8, are not gender delineated. Accept the complementarian conclusion if you can; I simply cannot. With an ever-growing number of Bible students who accept equality and mutuality of males and females in both the home and the church, I embrace both the surface and deeper levels of Galatians 3:28, a most pivotal text. If God's family is to reflect a piece of heaven on earth, how could it be otherwise?

What Should Progress in Spiritual Relationships Look Like?

I think Jesus' example helps answer this question concerning what progress looks like. Although I will say more about this in Chapter 7, Jesus' relationships with women were as countercultural as could be imagined. Women supported him financially. They traveled in his entourage. They sat at his feet to be taught, right along with the men. Actions like these would have been almost unthinkable even to Jewish folks, especially leaders.

Jesus had all authority given to him, yet he shared it with his apostles and followers for the purpose of saving the world (Matthew 28:18–20). But long before that, he sent the apostles out and then seventy others with authority to imitate him in performing all sorts of miracles. He was so anxious to share his leadership with others to serve the world that they must have been about as shocked as the series *The Chosen* depicts them. Leadership for Jesus was about servanthood, not authority and power over others. That was best left to the Gentile, non-Christian world, said he.

I dearly love reading about how his shared leadership progressed as described in two verses in John's Gospel. John 13:13 states: "You call me 'Teacher' and 'Lord,' and rightly so, for that is what I am." But were those roles his favorite way of describing his relationship with the apostles? Evidently not. "I no longer call you servants, because a servant does not know his master's business. Instead, I have called you friends, for everything that I learned from my Father I have made known to you" (John 15:15). Thus, for Jesus it was all about shared leadership for a shared mission. Might this have implications for the kind of relationship a husband and wife should have in shared equality, shared leadership, and friendship? Should this not describe the kind of relationships parents and children grow into?

Does a parent/child relationship stay the same over time? It stayed much the same in the biblical setting in several ways, given the rule of primogeniture. Generally, the new wife left her family and joined that of the new husband, for his *pater familias* (head of household in Roman culture) was still the dominant culture in the expanded family. Unsurprisingly, God presented a blow to what he knew patriarchy was going to become when he said, "That is why a man leaves his father and mother and is united to his wife, and they become one flesh" (Genesis 2:24). You will find many examples of God casting shade on patriarchy and its partner, primogeniture if you are looking. This is but the first.

When I got married at the ripe old age of 22, my father took off his "dad hat" and put on his "friend hat" in our relationship. Although he wasn't yet very spiritually minded (he was later), he was imitating Jesus, whether he realized it or not. After that transition, we related joyfully as two adults with one another. His action healed our damaged relationship almost immediately. All healthy relationships move in the direction of maturity, and thus equality.

How Should This Work with Wives and Husbands?

With the context above, I have a different understanding than I once did of Ephesians 5:21. "Submit to one another out of reverence for Christ." Many males, and some females, look at the verses following this one as an ordering of the marriage relationship with the wife submitting to the husband's authority. It seems we often love the idea of authority, even though Jesus said to replace it with servanthood. Those reading this with their patriarchal lenses on may be accusing me of exaggeration about now, and I understand why. I am spilling much ink to set the context of this passage to help us understand not just the passage, but to understand Jesus and true spiritual leadership.

Those with patriarchal glasses often exaggerate their conclusions to the point of being both unbiblical and illogical. In the "Complementarian Bible," one point is emphasized repeatedly in every way possible. The husband is the ultimate authority in the family and must make the final decisions for his family. Of course, it is said that he should take into consideration the opinions of other family members, but because he is the husband, final decisions are his to make.

> And both husband and wife should agree on the principle that the husband's decision should rightly hold sway if it does not involve sin.[38]

From this principle, both unbiblical and illogical conclusions flow. Let's start with their explanation regarding the initiation of sex within marriage. "A feminine initiation is in effect an invitation for the man to do his kind of initiating. In one sense then you could say that in those times the man is responding. But in fact, the wife is inviting him to lead in a way as only a man can, so that she can respond to him."[39] When I read that one, I couldn't help exclaiming my shock aloud. Here is what the Bible says about the matter in 1 Corinthians 7:3–4: "The husband should fulfill his marital duty to his wife, and likewise the wife to her husband. The wife does not have authority over her own body but yields it to her husband. In the same way, the husband does not have authority over his own body but yields it to his wife."

I'm just glad my wife read 1 Corinthians 7 and not Piper's com-

---

38. Grudem, *Recovering*, 40.

39. Grudem, *Recovering*, 40.

mentary. In marriage retreats through the years, we often used the example of an occasional occurrence in our marriage. At times, Theresa would initiate sex when I wasn't feeling well and when I told her how I was feeling, she would tilt her head slightly to one side and ask, with a twinkle in her eye, "Just how sick are you?" At this point, I almost always managed a chuckle and replied, "Well, I ain't dead yet!" This interchange was followed by a period of feeling much better, if only for a short while! Bottom line, if you are unwilling to shed your patriarchy, you will inevitably end up saying some weird stuff that actually contradicts the Bible, as I believe Piper did in this case.

A More Damaging, but Somewhat Logical Application

If the husband is indeed given the responsibility to make the final decisions in the physical family setting, producing in that case a one-man show, it would give credence to a similar decision-making process in the spiritual family setting. I believe this patriarchal, hierarchical view of how it should work in the physical family strongly influenced how it worked in the latter within congregations in our movement of churches in the early days. Need I say that it still operates that way in many, practically speaking, and inevitably tends in that direction by default because it is in our movement DNA.

Within the last year (2023), I talked to both elders and ministry staff who say that their "Lead Evangelist" (we love those titles, don't we?) leads in precisely that way—he makes the final decisions for the church, often without the knowledge or agreement of other leaders. Such leaders will usually say that they at least "bounced the ideas off of other leaders," but who are those other leaders? Too often, they are those chosen by the guy in the top position, because they think much the same as him or are afraid to voice differences—"yes guys."

I not only believe the complementarian view applied to church decision-making is damaging, I believe it also is within marriage.

How can final decision-making be determined by gender and not by gifts? It is a good thing that the wife in many marriages handles the finances. If she has expertise in that area, please give the woman the checkbook (or the online banking password). Otherwise, some tragedies will inevitably unfold. Somehow, complementarians have managed to let that one in the door, logically (and thankfully), although they still see it as the husband giving her permission so that his headship is maintained.

But what about other areas? In many marriages, the woman may be more intelligent than her husband. For example, I know wives who are far better educated than their husbands and work in managerial jobs, with expertise in all sorts of leadership and decision-making settings. They are better equipped to make final decisions in many areas than are their mates. But for the dedicated complementarian, gender must still settle it. That, to me, is simply astounding. We have two problems here. One is the lack of logic and common sense. The other is a rejection of all that Jesus teaches us through his own example about relationships maturing into teamwork and servanthood.

When he was about to leave the earth and leave the earthly mission in the hands of the Twelve, Jesus outlined that mission in the most basic of terms. They were to start in Jerusalem, go to Judea, Samaria, and to the ends of the earth (Acts 1:8). Wow! Now who's going to be making the decisions? Indirectly, one could say it was Jesus through the Holy Spirit, but even a casual reading of the NT shows just how indirect it really was most of the time. God's leaders were still creatures of choice, and so many choices were still left up to them (with the guidance of the Spirit, of course).

Here's How It Looks in My Marriage

We started off as a very young married couple, both raised in Louisiana. I was a full-fledged male chauvinist, no doubt about it. I didn't know much Bible, but I had the commonly accepted view of Ephesians 5:22–24 down pat. Theresa hated the word submission.

We have said many times, in seriousness, that had we both not loved sex, we might not have made it past the first six months. Thankfully, God soon invaded me and our marriage. I wasn't looking for him, but he was looking for me, and the details of how he brought it all together belong in the realm of the miraculous or near-miraculous. I became a fairly spiritual complementarian, and in time, a much more spiritual one. But I still looked at Genesis 3:16 as prescriptive and of course, Ephesians 5 through that same lens.

For years in teaching marriage retreats, I explained how we made decisions as something along these lines. We discussed the decisions to be made, and sometimes she convinced me of her view and sometimes I convinced her of my view. If we ended up at a stalemate, as the husband with final authority, I broke the tie and made the decisions. Then as I was starting to discuss the role of women in the home and the church with Jeanie Shaw, after I got over my initial hierarchical emotional reactions to her writing, something dawned on me.

I wasn't really the one breaking the ties when we had differing opinions, even in minor decisions, much less the major ones. We figured out a long time ago that breaking the tie regarding minor ones shouldn't take much time and energy at all. On such decisions, like which restaurant we will go to for a meal, we each pick a number between 1 and 10 and whoever's number is highest, they break the stalemate. After all, we eat over a thousand meals a year. How important could any one of them be anyway?

Then on the major decisions, I'm not about to break a tie, knowing that major decisions usually carry major consequences, especially if a decision turns out to be a bad one. In those cases, we get with other spiritual couples who have experience in the area of our potential decision, and they help us come to a decision we both feel good about. If you stop and think about it, one-person decisions are rather dumb when it is so easy to get advice from many counselors and advisors (Proverbs 15:22).

My wife is better equipped to make decisions in some areas

than I am, and vice versa. When that is the case, and I am wise enough to recognize it I just say, "That's your wheelhouse, you decide." She does the same with me. How did we get to this point of teamwork? Mutual respect and servanthood. Through this biblical principle of pragmatism, we discover what works best as God reveals it: "All of us, then, who are mature should take such a view of things. And if on some point you think differently that too God will make clear to you. Only let us live up to what we have already attained" (Philippians 3:15–16). Time, experience, spirituality, and discipling blended together create the formula that led us to the ultimate formula of teamwork, the shared responsibility in decision-making. The quality of my 59 years of marriage led me to write a book about our marriage entitled, *Fairy Tales Do Come True.*

Is my wife following what Ephesians 5 says she should do? Absolutely and amazingly! Am I following what the passage says I should do? I'm trying and I'm improving, but the husband's part is to me often overwhelming. Her part is submission to a sometimes knothead (me)! My part is following Jesus to the extremes of sacrifice, also submission. Whew! Husbands who are quick to go to Ephesians 5 to claim their manly authority are missing the point on mutual submission, the call to unity, and the necessity of self-sacrifice. Without question, both wives and husbands are presented with a mighty tall mountain to climb, a mountain that can only be scaled with great amounts of humility on both parts, thus attracting God's essential help.

The question will always remain about the original context of passages like Ephesians 5. Is the husband/wife relationship described here reflective of a principle for all time and all generations, or one described within a particular cultural setting and therefore not necessarily applicable to all future settings? I don't see how anyone can be absolutely certain either way. If it cannot be determined with certainty, that would automatically place it into the realm of an opinion matter. But rather than debate what appears to be an uncertain matter, let's just focus on the marvelous truths taught in the passage itself, for those definitely apply to all generations.

So where do we end this discussion of Ephesians 5? Right where we began. "Submit to one another out of reverence for Christ." This calls me to a renunciation of authority, control, and power, replacing it with submission to the needs of my wife and to her God-given set of gifts and experiences. This leads us to a brand of teamwork and shared responsibilities as friends of the forever variety. It's really a nice place to end up; I urge you to try it.

Chapter 6

A New Testament Perspective: Part 3: The Two Most Fundamental "Problem" Passages

A s we move from Ephesians 5, let us consider two other passages in the NT that have become the battleground regarding the women's role, yet they are simpler to navigate. The context surrounding 1 Corinthians 14:34–35 sheds light on its meaning. Let's look at these verses.

1 Corinthians 14:34–35
[34] Women should remain silent in the churches. They are not allowed to speak, but must be in submission, as the law says. [35] If they want to inquire about something, they should ask their own husbands at home; for it is disgraceful for a woman to speak in the church.

In that same broader context of 1 Corinthians, women were prophesying. The previous verses in 1 Corinthians 11 show clearly that women were both praying and prophesying, though they were to observe cultural norms for hair and head coverings as they did so. The discussion also included cultural norms for men as they prayed and prophesied. In the context, we see that praying and prophesying by both men and women were taking place in the same setting—the church. There is absolutely no indication that women were only leading these worship activities in women's groups. Quite the contrary. Bottom line, the predictions of Joel 2, as quoted in Acts 2, were being fulfilled. It is interesting to me that while we have easily shed the veil instructions from this passage, it is still part of our culture for men to take their hats off when they pray. If they feel obliged to do that, shouldn't they take them off and hand them to their wives to put on? (smile...)

It is difficult to deny that these predictions about prophesying were carried out in this context. Thankfully, few still try to deny them, although some will try to water down definitions of the term prophesy. Furthermore, the Greek term translated "silent" in verse 34 means *absolutely silent,* and if generally applied to all women they could not even sing. Plus, whoever these women were, they had husbands. So it seems relatively certain that they were the wives of men participating in the service, likely those who were prophesying. It should also be noted that although the Greek term translated "women" here, *gune,* can be translated as either women or wives, contextually it would have made more sense to translate it as wives. I just don't spend much time on this one, since trying to apply it the way some do is such a great stretch beyond the context.

Whether in 1 Corinthians or 1 Timothy, the fact remains that some women were veering outside socially accepted norms and were thus bringing undue attention to the spiritual life of the church. The most likely reason was found in society and how some women were going beyond the accepted lines of behavior. However, the reason could have been traced back to a condition that arose within the church. As you read Peppiatt's explanation below, you will have to admit that it fits the human tendency to take a good thing too far. It is worth considering. If accurate, it would provide a helpful way to view both our 1 Corinthians passage and 1 Timothy 2.

The dominant picture among scholars is a version of the following: Christian women converts who have been brought up in a blatantly misogynist society, freed by their newfound relationship with Jesus Christ into a reconstituted way of relating to the world, to men, and to one another, taught by Paul that in Christ there is no longer a superior/inferior relationship between male and female, licensed by Paul to pray and prophesy, and invited even to lead, have been corrupted, and are beginning to behave in disgraceful ways. In this newfound existence, initially encouraged by Paul, they have veered into shameful (even disgusting) practices.[40]

To be fair, Peppiatt herself doesn't agree with this dominant picture she describes. She believes what the title of her book suggests, that much of Paul's argumentation in this section of 1 Corinthians is rhetorical in nature as he writes:

1 Corinthians 14:34–36
[34] Women should remain silent in the churches. They are not allowed to speak, but must be in submission, as the law says. [35] If they want to inquire about something, they should ask their own husbands at home; for it is disgraceful for a woman to speak in the church. [36] Or did the word of God originate with you? Or are you the only people it has reached?

Peppiatt suggests that Paul is quoting what some were teaching falsely and rhetorically refuting it. No doubt Paul uses this approach in passages like 1 Corinthians 8:1, 10:23 and others. In 1 Corinthians 14, Paul could then be in verses 34–35 quoting those who object to women's participation, and in verse 36 ("Did the word of God originate with you?") rebuking them to defend women's participation. I'm not persuaded of that interpretation, but given her reputation as a voracious reader of writings on the topic at hand, I value her assessment of the dominant viewpoint of scholarship in general. She states it well.

---

40. Lucy Peppiatt, *Women and Worship at Corinth: Paul's Rhetorical Arguments in 1 Corinthains* (Eugene, OR: Cascade Books, 2015), 40. Kindle.

What About 1 Corinthians 11:3, 7–12?

[3] But I want you to realize that the head of every man is Christ, and the head of the woman is man, and the head of Christ is God... [7] A man ought not to cover his head, since he is the image and glory of God; but woman is the glory of man. [8] For man did not come from woman, but woman from man; [9] neither was man created for woman, but woman for man. [10] It is for this reason that a woman ought to have authority over her own head, because of the angels. [11] Nevertheless, in the Lord woman is not independent of man, nor is man independent of woman. [12] For as woman came from man, so also man is born of woman. But everything comes from God.

The context here still shows women praying and prophesying. Joel 2 and Acts 2 still read the same. Whatever else may be said, Paul's unusual observations here support the cultural appropriateness to be followed by both men and women in the passage. It is an unusual passage, as the following quote shows, making it a precipitous endeavor if applying it in any other context with any other application.

> The occasional and contextual nature of Paul's choice of wording in this verse is important to notice. It is evident that the meaning of the term "head" in the paired formulations of 11:3 seems to be created for this particular section since it is found in this connection nowhere else in Paul's writings. Specifically, Paul nowhere else uses this term "head" (kephalē) to denote the relationship between Christ and every male. Nor is there corroborating evidence elsewhere in Paul for his use of this word to depict the relationship between men and women. Most significantly, in all the Christological formulas and texts in Paul there are none which use the terminology of head to talk about the relationship between God and Christ.[41]

---

41. "The College Press NIV Commentary," Wordsearch Electronic Edition, 1 Cor. 11.

N.T. Wright is most likely correct in defining "head" in this verse.

> But what does Paul mean by 'head'? He uses it here sometimes in a metaphorical sense, as in verse 3, and sometimes literally, as when he's talking about what to do with actual human heads (verses 4–7 and 10). But the word he uses can mean various different things; and a good case can be made out for saying that in verse 3 he is referring not to 'headship' in the sense of sovereignty, but to 'headship' in the sense of 'source', like the 'source' or 'head' of a river. In fact, in some of the key passages where he explains what he's saying (verses 8, 9 and 12a) he is referring explicitly to the creation story in Genesis 2, where woman was made from the side of man.[42]

Unsurprisingly then, this verse is not addressing authority, God over Christ, or man over woman. Both men and women were addressed equally as needing to stay within cultural boundaries as they participated in public worship. The term *Christ,* or *Messiah,* designates a human role for Jesus as a man. Paul does not say God was the head of the eternal *Logos* (John 1), but of Christ, his only Son whom he gave for the redemption of the world. Philippians 2:6 has something to say about the topic, for in eternity Jesus was "in very nature God" and "did not consider equality with God something to be used to his own advantage." This is compelling evidence that the term "head" is a reference to source. Adam was the source of Eve, via his rib (side, actually) and the two of them as male and female were the *imago Dei* of their Maker.

In 1 Corinthians 11:11–12, Paul sums up the mutuality and interdependence of male and female, to protect against drawing conclusions beyond his original purpose in using his analogies. Wright was not wrong when he stated in the same paper just quoted that aside from the teaching of men and women both participating

---

42. N.T. Wright, "Women's Service in the Church: The Biblical Basis, St. John's College, Durham, Sept 4, 2004, a conference paper for the Symposium, "Men, Women, and the Church."

in public worship, almost everything else in the passage seemed remarkably difficult to nail down. This fact puts it in the realm of opinion matters, not doctrinal matters. Paul brings it back to an important concluding thought here, which many feel Paul does in a clever way of writing to make his point that in Christ, it is not about who came from whom or who has the authority.

For those who do take 1 Corinthians 11:3 to indicate authority, how can it be limited to men and women in the church? The statements are very broad—the head of woman is man, period. If this verse is a reflection of Genesis 3:16, as it would be if placed in the realm of determining authority, it should be applied to all women, in and out of the church, and to women in all settings. If not, why not? At the least, you would have to admit that the principle prohibits all women from having authority over all men, and even though women in the world are violating it, we should do our best to prohibit Christian women from violating it. Thus, they should not occupy any role in the world that would place them in authority over a male. Some in the past have taught exactly this as they insisted on being both literal in interpretation and logical in application. I don't see any way of avoiding this conclusion if the authoritative over/under principle is really the correct interpretation of the verse. Do you?

1 Timothy 2:11–14

[11] A woman should learn in quietness and full submission. [12] I do not permit a woman to teach or to assume authority over a man; she must be quiet. [13] For Adam was formed first, then Eve. [14] And Adam was not the one deceived; it was the woman who was deceived and became a sinner.

This passage is a much more challenging one than 1 Corinthians 14, to be sure. Verse 11 sets the stage for what is about to be forbidden, but not in ways you might first assume. All students were to learn in quietness and submission to the teacher, both male and female. Learning from a rabbi or teacher was seen as a real privilege, and until the church was established, a privilege not often offered to women. The account of Mary and Martha in Luke 10 shows how unusual it was for a woman to sit at a rabbi's feet to learn. Martha's frustration at what her sister was doing is understandable from a cultural standpoint. Mary was doing something quite out of the ordinary in Jewish circles, whereas Martha was doing what was commonly expected of a woman. This is just another example of how Jesus was loosening the bonds of patriarchy, accepted customs notwithstanding.

The real verse at issue here is verse 12. It is very important to note that the Greek term for exercising authority here (*authenteô*) is used only here in the New Testament. It would seem clear that the normal concept of authority is not being addressed. Otherwise, the usual term for authority would have been used. That said, the lexicons don't agree on how the word is to be taken in the passage. The Greek construction indicates that whatever meaning is chosen, it also affects the idea of "teach" in this verse. They are clearly connected. "Teach" would then be understood either as "authoritative teaching" or "domineering or independent authoritative teaching." Three considerations lead me to the definition of domineering teaching.

One, the Temple of Diana was the cultural center of the city, and in this magnificent structure and its pagan worship, women priestesses were front and center in their influence and leadership. Two, when you add in the feminist movement of its day in this city, no doubt spurred on by the temple and its feminine influences and the New Roman Women Movement thought to be prevalent in Greco-Roman cultures, this would signal a breakout from women's cultural standards of past years. To assume that women in the church would be tempted to brazenly thrust themselves into roles like many women in that society were doing would likely be a significant understatement.

Three, the broader context of the verse in question would encompass the three Pastoral Epistles. The type of authoritative, corrective teaching Paul calls the evangelists to use would raise the question about women teaching in this manner in that society at the time, and perhaps in any other age, including ours. Perhaps 1 Timothy 2:12 might well have been aimed at this issue, concluding that it would be inappropriate for women to do this type of disciplinary, corrective teaching in that cultural setting. The question of whether this would be acceptable in any church setting today would depend on the nature of that culture, for cultures around our present world vary greatly.

This question calls us to consider the specific church roles to which women could be appointed. Any mention of broadened functions of women in worship services, like teaching or praying unaccompanied by the presence of a man, almost always leads to people asking this question: "Are you saying that a woman can be an elder or a lead evangelist?" Culture still plays a part in answering this question, and even in America, what might work in Oregon may not work in Arkansas.

My bigger question is why we feel so motivated to ask that question in the first place. Most of our members, including most of our leaders, have not studied the issue deeply enough and with genuinely open minds to reach the proverbial first base, so why are we so anxious to address the possibility of sliding into home plate? Curiosity you may say? Yes, but curiosity perhaps born of the patriarchy in which we have been steeped, often unaware. Might the questions and fears be rooted in concerns for who is going to have the power, the control? Patriarchy strikes again and again, and again. If we had more often experienced the type of male servant leadership which Jesus spoke about in Matthew 20, we would be far less concerned about leadership roles of women.

For now, let's just focus on getting to first base, providing the opportunities to females in the church that the New Testament provides. The rest will become clear with time as we implement what we are quite late implementing already. When we start with what should be clear, the rest of the path God will make clear in his time. That is what Philippians 3:15–16 teaches, so let's trust the principle that God has provided to us repeatedly through the years, both individually and collectively.

The gender issue also comes into question when comparing the "now" phase of the kingdom between husbands and wives, which will continue to be relegated to the "now only" phase, since marrying and being given in marriage will remain a part of the "not yet" (heaven) stage. Whether we retain our maleness and femaleness as a part of our personality in heaven of who we are now, based on our earthly personality, is an unanswered question. In Galatians 3:28, two of the three relationships can be like the ultimate stage of heaven in the here and now. Freed slaves in most settings (America being somewhat different due to the race/color factor) can totally blend in so that there is neither slave nor free, and the same applies to Jews and Gentiles. Whatever may be the case in the afterlife regarding males and females, what Paul said in Galatians 3 is good enough for me in the present. I've experienced enough precious relationships with God's daughters to understand the relationships Jesus and Paul had with their spiritual women friends of their day, and I'm not about to diminish those experiences in my life or theirs in any manner whatsoever.

And What About the Ending of the Chapter?

Again I ask, what about it? Here it is.

1 Timothy 2:13–15 (NASB)

[13] For it was Adam who was first created, and then Eve. [14] And it was not Adam who was deceived, but the woman being deceived, fell into transgression. [15] But women will be preserved through the bearing of children if they continue in faith and love and sanctity with self-restraint.

Let's begin with the first verse regarding the order of creation. The assumption is often made that being created last somehow shows that Eve is in some way inferior to Adam. If you go back to the creation account itself, what do you find about the progressive order of all other parts of that original creation? It moves from the simpler to the more complex. In that sense, each successive part of creation becomes an improvement over the previous one. Do you really think that this changed with the creation of humans? I decidedly do not. I will give but a few reasons for believing the well-established progression continued.

Females have not come close to exercising the destructive power exerted by males since the dawn of time. Females are often more relationship oriented than are men, and if God created humans to enjoy relationships with him in time and eternity, many women seem to have gotten the better part of that divine design. Three, the order of creation did go from simpler to more complex throughout the whole creative sequence. Which male will argue that females are not more complex than males (to add a bit of humor)? It does seem to be the case that the Holy Spirit worked in both the physical creation and the spiritual creation in following a path which was progressive, not digressive. Four, aside from physical size and strength, are men superior to women? Women have been granted the unbelievable privilege of bringing forth their own human creations through the process of procreation. Yes, the man plays his part, but it pales in comparison to the woman's part. A bond is built by having a baby develop inside the mother's own body and that child remains almost totally dependent on her throughout infanthood and early childhood, especially in the patriarchal setting that has dominated human history. For humankind, this often created a bond to the mother stronger than the bond between man and his progeny. The old saying that the hand that rocks the cradle rules the world didn't become popular for no reason. I'm not arguing that this should be the case; I'm arguing that it is far more often the case than not.

From Genesis 3:16 forward, the development of male and female roles was clearly set in motion in certain directions. Men, being larger and stronger, would find their roles in the fields and on the battlegrounds. Women would have the babies and raise them, and without birth control, that role would be firmly entrenched for most of their years prior to middle-age. By then, grandmotherhood was in place and the same roles would continue. These lifelong experiences would naturally develop more of a nurturing character in them. The men, especially considering the large numbers that ended up on the battlefield, would develop quite a different nature. We may have invented the terminology for PTSD, but we by no means invented the malady. Patriarchy took care of that one.

Jesus lived his earthly sojourn in a patriarchal setting, and from this vantage point he almost exclusively addressed male leadership and the tendency to dominate. Most of his rebukes and corrections were directed toward males, even outside of leadership considerations. He dealt with those root sins repeatedly in his chosen apostles. I don't read of similar corrections dished out to the women who followed him, which is something worth contemplating.

Paul's Purpose in This Example?

Men often practice domineering postures, living up to the rough and powerful image they can often feel is their expectation and right. But why did Paul address the creation order in this letter? I believe it is for the same reason that he states that Eve was the first one deceived. It fit his purpose. Some of the women in the church were being deceived by the cultural concepts surrounding them and needed to wake up. The application Paul made of the Genesis account was suited to provide that wake-up call. In other passages, the focus of sin's entrance into the world was centered on Adam's part in it.

The Bible gives different instructions and scenarios for different purposes. David, the man after God's own heart in one context was also the man who broke God's heart in another. The very first mention of him in the New Testament, only six verses in, is this: "David was the father of Solomon, whose mother had been Uriah's wife…" (Matthew 1:6). This verse conjures up the most horrible period of David's entire life. Not such a grand entrance for him upon whose throne the Messiah was to sit. We can then read in Matthew 12:3–4 where Jesus used the example of David in a good way, though as a Law breaker, evidently with God's approval. In Acts 13:12, he was called a man after God's own heart. Did any of these polar opposite examples establish some eternal principle, and if so, which was it—the good or the bad example of David?

We can also read of Moses, the one whose name is attached to the Law of God, for it is most often called the Law of Moses. Numbers 12:3 provides us with this startling statement about him: "Now Moses was a very humble man, more humble than anyone else on the face of the earth." That very same Moses laid aside that mantle of humility and in rebellion to God committed a sin serious enough to block him from entering the Promised Land. Acts 7 describes the murder he committed in killing an Egyptian and then his flight out of Egypt to live in the desert until his courage had all but dried up. He had to have his brother accompany him back into Egypt before he became the leader he was to become. Which version of Moses do we focus on, the good or the bad? Is either example intended to be used as some kind of eternal principle or are both to be used to illustrate the contextual examples needed?

Obviously, examples can be used for different applications, as can statements. Jesus, in one context said, "for whoever is not against us is for us" (Matthew 9:40), and in another he said the opposite, "Whoever is not with me is against me…" (Luke 11:23). Is that a contradiction or merely a different application called for in different settings? In 1 Corinthians 7:8, Paul said it was good for the unmarried and widows to stay unmarried, yet in 1 Timothy 5:14 he counseled younger widows to marry. A contradiction? Will we ever learn to allow biblical writers to use examples and statements as specific contexts demand without trying to use them to establish some ongoing principle for all generations? If the texts themselves do not make it clear that such are intended to establish eternal principles, what gives us the right to do so?

Given that Satan is the great deceiver, and his first deception of humans was with Eve, it should not be surprising that Paul uses her twice to warn women who were being deceived by Satan through their culture and the false teachers within it (2 Corinthians 11:3; 1 Timothy 2:14).

Paul, at the least, in using *authenteô* to denote a seizing of power or authority, is forbidding an action that neither women nor men should be taking. Whatever the case, he is pointing out that as in Genesis 3, at least some women in Ephesus were being deceived like Eve had been and should wake up to that fact and repent. Both Adam and Eve sinned. Here, Eve's part is focused on in a New Testament passage, and in other New Testament passages, Adam's part was the focus. Nothing beyond what is mentioned should be made of an illustration that was used this one time. It is not a theological statement from which other applications are to be derived. Of course, those immersed with patriarchy-imbued theology will be tempted to use it to further implicate females with some sort of inherent inferiority.

Most of the examples from the Old Testament used in the New Testament are negative examples. What difference does it make if the example comes from Genesis 3 or Genesis 4, including Cain killing his brother, or the various sins associated with Lot in Genesis 19? 2 Peter 2:7 uses Lot as a righteous example. The fact that sinful examples are used from the first book of the Bible doesn't establish some permanent principle for all time unless it is so stated. In Matthew 19:8 and parallel Gospel accounts, Jesus answered a question about divorce by saying, "But it was not this way from the beginning." In this case, although he allowed exceptions, his original ideal will is stated. All sinful examples from all parts of the Bible are applied in a specific New Testament setting for a specific reason that applied simply to that particular setting. Any attempt to make it a permanent principle is purely an assumption, unless the text itself makes that application, as does Matthew 19.

I believe such assumptions arise from two basic mistakes. One is the power of patriarchy, and the other is the faulty system of hermeneutics (biblical interpretation) which we have inherited from our forefathers of the Restoration Movement. In neither case do we realize what is influencing our thinking, for it has become so natural that we simply don't see it—until we do. May God help us to reach that stage!

Let's Hit the Pause Button

About now, in my writing I am feeling great empathy for Eve. How would you like it if you were remembered for your first and worst sin? That was not the intent of the biblical record, but it is what we have done to her for centuries. We have taken a snapshot of her at her worst and paraded her around as an example of women at their worst to diminish the female gender rather than see them as Genesis introduces Eve before sin entered the world. She was fully portrayed as Adam's equal. Equality and mutuality reigned supreme. Adam needed her and was incomplete without her.

Then they both sinned and sinned grievously, and we, if we follow our self-righteous, judgmental spirits fail to see the rest of their lives or imagine the guilt with which they lived when they realized that what they had done would bring horrific and irreversible consequences on this planet's inhabitants until time ends. They had to watch those consequences play out in their own family as their firstborn son, whose birth no doubt brought them the same great delight that the births of our children do, killed their righteous second-born son. No parent should live to see their children die before them, we say, but they saw it in the most tragic way possible.

But the couple didn't stay hidden nor did they give up. Evidently, they repented and learned from their sins. Would we have done better? Do we do better, knowing so much more about Satan than they possibly could have known when they sinned? They had another son, who proved to be exemplary, and surely good parenting had something to do with that as they continued to repent and learn. Read it.

Genesis 5:3–4
³ When Adam had lived 130 years, he had a son in his own likeness, in his own image; and he named him Seth.
⁴ After Seth was born, Adam lived 800 years and had other sons and daughters.

Genesis 4:25–26
²⁵ Adam made love to his wife again, and she gave birth to a son and named him Seth, saying, "God has granted me another child in place of Abel, since Cain killed him."
²⁶ Seth also had a son, and he named him Enosh. At that time people began to call on the name of the LORD.

As you can tell, I think we (not the Bible) have done a great disservice to both Adam and Eve in focusing on their first and worst sin, something we would loathe to have done to us. Yes, God had the inspired writers use their example to help us more fully understand the big picture and our stories in theirs, but he also had inspired writers share their best days before that sin in the Garden and their better days after it. Yet for centuries, in the case of Eve, we have only focused on her worst day and used it in ways that can make feel women feel like second class citizens at best, rather than looking at the Bible as a whole to understand and appreciate the beautiful daughters of God, all of whom trace their origin back to a woman named Eve, God's very first daughter. How would you like your daughter to have been made such a public negative spectacle, with all eyes focused on the worst moment in her life? Thank you, Eve, for not giving up. Thank you for showing us that by God's grace, life goes on after we sin. If we knew the rest of your story, as we one day will, we might see you as a hero rather than as a failure. It's time we hit that pause button and do some deeper thinking and soul-searching.

One Certainty Remains

We continually see women shine throughout Scripture. The promise in Joel 2 and Acts 2 came to pass in the early church. Women prophesied. They prophesied to mixed audiences. Jesus paved the way for women in his kingdom through his earthly ministry. As I view the scriptures concerning how women should function in both the home and the church, I now have the conviction that anything a man can do in a church service, a woman can also do. The appointment to the specific roles of elder or congregational evangelist is an unsettled question for me at present, but I've not stopped considering the issue. As one of my more progressive friends says, women have been functioning as elders in many settings for decades. Who can deny it? And as I have often said, in many situations where the woman is more gifted, I would much prefer to listen to the gifted woman rather than the less-gifted man. In none of the NT passages describing spiritual gifts do I see gender playing a role.

Women in the present society of my country have few limitations in what they can do. It seems odd, actually wrong, to me that their opportunities outside the church are virtually limitless, yet inside the church still quite limited, often in ways that seem demeaning and hurtful to them when the scriptures in their context say otherwise. Sisters, I am sorry. I want to help and I'm trying to help. I recently heard the story of a women in one of our churches that illustrates this point all too well. She is a well-known and well-respected professor in an outstanding university who has spoken before the legislature of her state. In seeking how she could use her gifts, education, and experiences to best serve in the church, she learned that she could usher and teach in the children's ministry. God help us! I will just let Paul's observations close out this chapter.

1 Corinthians 9:19–22

Though I am free and belong to no one, I have made myself a slave to everyone, to win as many as possible. [20] To the Jews I became like a Jew, to win the Jews. To those under the law I became like one under the law (though I myself am not under the law), so as to win those under the law. [21] To those not having the law I became like one not having the law (though I am not free from God's law but am under Christ's law), so as to win those not having the law. [22] To the weak I became weak, to win the weak. I have become all things to all people so that by all possible means I might save some. 🌱

Chapter 7

An Overall Biblical Perspective: God Highlighted Women

The foundation for the first part of this book is unmistakable and must be kept in mind when considering any aspect of the role of women in the church and in the home. Genesis 3:16 was descriptive of what the entrance of sin into the world would produce—calamity and chaos from that point forward as the desire for power and control permeated the human race, particularly the male population. Therefore, God's purpose after the Fall was redemptive and preparatory for his ultimate goal of enjoying the closest relationship possible with the humanity he had created. This purpose demanded that he increasingly confront patriarchy and primogeniture as he moved the human race toward eternity with him. The now/not yet aspects of his kingdom will be progressing throughout history until the heavenly kingdom has swallowed up all earlier phases.

Learning to Expect the Unexpected

Isaiah included two verses that should prepare us for experiencing the unexpected in almost all interactions with God.

Isaiah 55:8–9

[8] "For my thoughts are not your thoughts, neither are your ways my ways," declares the LORD. [9] "As the heavens are higher than the earth, so are my ways higher than your ways and my thoughts than your thoughts."

If humans had been the authors of the biblical record, they would have omitted many things that God included and included many things that God omitted. That would be true because God is divine and we are but human, but it would also be true because patriarchy is a part of our natural thinking and feeling process.

The first chapter of the New Testament begins with the genealogy of Jesus, forty-two generations. Normal genealogies of the day would have included only the names of men, not women. Matthew's account mentions five women, starting with Tamar, whose children were produced through a sordid relationship with her father-in-law, the founder of the tribe out of which Jesus would come. The next woman mentioned was Rahab, a non-Jewish prostitute. Then we read of Ruth, another non-Jew, a Moabitess. Jesus may have been a Jew, but physically, clearly not a pureblooded one. That raises the question in one's mind of how many Jews of Jesus' day might have rejected him on that basis alone, given their pride in the purity of their bloodlines.

We continue to read of Uriah's wife, Bathsheba, bringing to mind David's sins of adultery and murder, yet David was the one whose throne would ultimately be occupied by the Messiah himself. The list ends with the Messiah's mother, Mary, who was divinely pregnant out of wedlock; she would have been viewed as flawed from a human viewpoint, no doubt the fodder for immense speculation and gossip. Yes, in dealing with God, we learn to expect the unexpected as the flaws of heroes are placed in plain view and the accomplishments of non-heroes raised to hero status. Preaching about the latter types, Jesus was nearly killed for comparing a widow of Zarephath to widows in Israel and comparing Naaman, a foreigner from an enemy nation, to lepers in Israel (Luke 4:24–30). Examples abound of God going directly against the grain of human thinking. Pride in power and position failed the wisest man in the Old Testament, according to Ecclesiastes, and God was never short of approaches showing that his ways are not man's ways. Nor were his attacks against man's ways subtle, starting with the ones against the pride and power of primogeniture with its built-in misogyny.

Primogeniture Rejection

The very first human produced by the act of procreation, Cain, became the father of the ungodly lineage of his parents whereas his younger brother, Seth, became the father of the more spiritually inclined lineage. This constituted but the first divine blow of many to the rule of primogeniture, an important aspect of patriarchy's insidious control that granted privilege to the firstborn male. Abraham's firstborn, Ishmael, was not the son of promise, but rather his second-born, Isaac. Isaac had twin sons, Esau and Jacob. While the twins were still in Rebekah's womb, God said that the older would serve the younger. And so it came to pass through trickery that Jacob, the younger twin, became the inheritor of his father's blessing and his older brother's birthright.

Jacob's life became wrapped up in a tale of a female brand of primogeniture, intrigue, and deception. He was tricked by his father-in-law to marry the older sister rather than the younger whom he loved. The older got her husband first but not his heart, for the younger one had that secured before that first wedding night and the wild morning wakeup call. But Leah still became the progenitor of the tribe destined to produce the Christ, for God blessed her to be the mother of Judah and not the mother of the favored child destined to be a hero of heroes in Jewish history, Joseph, the son of Rachel. God ended up blessing both women in making their mark on history through their offspring. Both women were victims at the hand of their own father, but in other ways victorious through the intervention of their heavenly Father.

Tamar was impregnated by Judah, who thought she was a prostitute rather than his own daughter-in-law. Her pregnancy resulted in twins and an improbable story.

Genesis 38:27–30

[27] When the time came for her to give birth, there were twin boys in her womb. [28] As she was giving birth, one of them put out his hand; so the midwife took a scarlet

thread and tied it on his wrist and said, "This one came out first." [29] But when he drew back his hand, his brother came out, and she said, "So this is how you have broken out!" And he was named Perez. [30] Then his brother, who had the scarlet thread on his wrist, came out. And he was named Zerah.

Keeping with the pattern of striking blows against primogeniture, the one that was to be second-born displaced the one that was to be firstborn by coming out first. Thus, from Perez came the house of David as the lineage of Jesus developed. Genesis ends with the story of Joseph, the highly favored son in his father's heart and the highly blessed by his heavenly Father, yet he was the tenth removed from the firstborn son of the family, Reuben. Joseph's dreams came true, although he had no idea what they meant when he dreamed them. His brothers did in fact bow down to him, although they had initially hated and rejected him.

Finally, when Joseph brought his two sons Manasseh and Ephraim to his father Israel to bless them, Israel laid his hand on the head of the younger Ephraim. This caused a quick and negative reaction from Joseph.

Genesis 48:17–19

[17] When Joseph saw his father placing his right hand on Ephraim's head he was displeased; so he took hold of his father's hand to move it from Ephraim's head to Manasseh's head. [18] Joseph said to him, "No, my father, this one is the firstborn; put your right hand on his head." [19] But his father refused and said, "I know, my son, I know. He too will become a people, and he too will become great. Nevertheless, his younger brother will be greater than he, and his descendants will become a group of nations."

Thus closes the Genesis account and its recording of God's intent to deal with a primary inclination of sinful mankind to build social constructs that divide his creation rather than unite it. Many similar examples could be cited, such as David, the youngest of eight sons, and Solomon, likely the tenth son of his father David, being exalted to the kingship of God's nation. Primogeniture remains a force among social constructs, but it means nothing to God. He seemed as inclined to thwart it as Jesus was to violate Sabbath days with his miracles. What Jesus said to Peter on one occasion would fit most humans throughout biblical history, "You do not have in mind the concerns of God, but merely human concerns" (Mark 8:33).

Female Leadership in the OT—Deborah First

Champions of patriarchy have but one rationalization to offer when women leaders in the Bible are mentioned. They led only because there were no men willing to step up to their rightful place of leadership. Deborah is the poster child for this premise, and Barak is the failed masculine leader who should have been what he was not. As someone who both prides himself in being a biblically grounded teacher of Scripture and who has taught this very perversion of Scripture, I must begin by apologizing in my embarrassment. What the complementarians teach is what I forcefully taught when I was among their ranks. Thank the good Lord for time to keep learning and growing in knowledge and for opportunities to repent.

We will look at a number of other women leaders in the Bible, but it is most appropriate to begin with this example for two reasons. One, it is the poster child example most often used to explain away God's choice of leaders when their gender does not fit preconceived ideas. Two, it is clearly in violation of what has often been taught about women leaders being used because of men's failures of leadership, specifically, their refusals to lead. With that in mind, let's look at what the Bible says about this stellar biblical example of a powerful female leader.

Judges 4:4–10

[4] Now Deborah, a prophet, the wife of Lappidoth, was leading Israel at that time. [5] She held court under the Palm of Deborah between Ramah and Bethel in the hill country of Ephraim, and the Israelites went up to her to have their disputes decided. [6] She sent for Barak son of Abinoam from Kedesh in Naphtali and said to him, "The LORD, the God of Israel, commands you: 'Go, take with you ten thousand men of Naphtali and Zebulun and lead them up to Mount Tabor. [7] I will lead Sisera, the commander of Jabin's army, with his chariots and his troops to the Kishon River and give him into your hands.' " [8] Barak said to her, "If you go with me, I will go; but if you don't go with me, I won't go." [9] "Certainly I will go with you," said Deborah. "But because of the course you are taking, the honor will not be yours, for the LORD will deliver Sisera into the hands of a woman." So Deborah went with Barak to Kedesh. [10] There Barak summoned Zebulun and Naphtali, and ten thousand men went up under his command. Deborah also went up with him.

Much of what you learn about the ensuing battle is in the next chapter, in a song sung by the two featured leaders and heroes, Deborah and Barak. The Israelites were severely oppressed for twenty years by the Canaanites, whose king was Jabin and whose commander of the army was Sisera. Because of the oppression, God's people were afraid to travel except by way of backroads and countryside. Their army consisted of peasants and farmers, not a trained military force. They were called simply "villagers" in Judges 5:7. God had to choose new leaders, for it was said that "not a shield or spear was seen among forty thousand in Israel" (Judges 5:8). Some of the tribes sent volunteers but others were called out because they wouldn't join in the battle. It was far from an ideal setting in which to do battle against a real army, one that boasted

900 chariots fitted with iron, while Israel's army was composed of those who rode on donkeys or simply walked.

What does the biblical text tell us about Deborah and Barak? Let's start with Deborah. One, she was a prophet. Two, she was leading Israel. Three, she held court and made judgments for the Israelites who came to her with legal issues. Like Samuel, she was both prophet and judge, the only other person in the OT with that distinction. Four, as prophet and leader, she called Barak at God's direction to lead the army and prophesied what was going to happen in the battle, including the ultimate victory. (The next chapter provides the background of why God choose this battleground near the river Kishon. God sent a downpour of rain sufficient to cause the river to flood out of its banks and create havoc with those 900 chariots.) Five, Deborah was very courageous, answering Barak's request to accompany him in the battle with the words, "Certainly I will go with you" (Judges 4:9). If she was some type of substitute leader, she apparently was unaware of it, as was the entire nation.

Barak has been accused of being many unbecoming things as a leader, including being a weakling and a spineless coward. Grudem, unsurprisingly, says that the situation of Deborah "was a living indictment of the weakness of Barak and other men in Israel who should have been more courageous leaders (Judges 4:9)."[43] That is more than a bit shocking, given what Judges and Hebrews say about Barak. He is found in the roll call of heroes in Hebrews 11:32, along with the likes of Gideon, Samson, Jephthah, David, Samuel, and the prophets. Not bad company if you ask me (instead of Grudem).

What does Judges 4–5 say about him? One, he was directly chosen by God, according to the prophet, Deborah. Two, he was smart enough to ask the leader of Israel, a prophet and judge, to accompany him. Most likely he wanted assurance that what she said was commanded by God was in fact truly commanded, which

---

43. Grudem, *Recovering*, 72.

her willingness to enter the battle with him would have proven. Three, he led the Israelite army into the battle, although clearly outmanned. Four, once the opposing army started retreating, posing no other immediate threat, he still pursued them until every last man was killed. Five, he wasn't threatened by women leadership. In fact, he both sought it and praised it. His and Deborah's prophetic song in Judges 5 included this verse about Jael. "Most blessed of women be Jael, the wife of Heber the Kenite, most blessed of tent-dwelling women" (Judges 5:24).

The beginning of their song has in verse 2 an oft-quoted principle describing the ideal function of leadership and followership. "When the princes in Israel take the lead, when the people willingly offer themselves—praise the LORD!" The final verse has its own inspiration, as the leadership team of male and female sing, "So may all your enemies perish, LORD! But may all who love you be like the sun when it rises in its strength" (verse 31). The victorious conclusion led to peace in the land for forty years. Obviously, this is a story of faith, powerful leadership, and victory, not one of female exceptions and substitutions because of male cowardice and rejection of leadership. Such contrived stories are an affront to the characters involved and thus to the Bible itself. Give Deborah and Barak their due—they've more than earned it.

The First Female Prophet—Miriam

I have read many books on women's leadership and their proper roles in both home and church. All of them had some helpful information, although some much more than others. At this point, my two favorites have been *Malestrom* by Carolyn Custis James and *Women Serving God* by John Mark Hicks. The appeal to me of Hicks' book is threefold. One, his journey on the topic parallels mine almost exactly. I wrote a book about my spiritual journey entitled *My Three Lives*, and my journey on the women's topic has three stages also, just as John Mark's does. Two, Hicks is very analytical with striking logic that is difficult or impossible to dismiss.

Three, he has a biblical depth that impressively encompasses the text and historical contextual background.

Here are a few quotes from him as he introduces women leaders in the Old Testament:

> Does God ever empower women with gifts and authorize women to act in ways that violate the divine intent in creation? If not, then nothing women do in Israel that God authorizes violates whatever God intended in creation.
>
> As a beginning, here is an important fact. No text in the Hebrew Bible silences women in its assemblies.
>
> The first prophet named in the Torah is Abraham (Genesis 20:7). The second is Aaron (Exodus 7:1). The third is Miriam (Exodus 15:20). The fourth is Moses (Deuteronomy 18:15). That is an impressive list. She also makes another notable list, "I sent before you," God says, "Moses, Aaron, and Miriam" (Micah 6:4). The Exodus was led by Moses, Aaron, and Miriam. This sibling trio was commissioned to lead the people of God ("I sent"), and God gifted them for this mission. All three were prophets.[44]

From there, Hicks goes on to show that Miriam led the first communal worship assembly in song after the exodus from Egypt. Did her brother Moses need to stand at her side while she led singing? Nothing in the text would indicate such. In fact, nothing in any text, OT or NT, indicates such. The practice of having a man stand beside a woman any time she is in front of the church for any type of sharing is an invention. I described some of those inventions in chapter 2 under the heading of pattern or blueprint theology. Interestingly, it is even one step removed from that, making a pattern of an assumed principle drawn from an assumed pattern. Confused yet? Don't worry—I'm confused too, since I can find neither the example of the practice nor the principle supposedly behind it. Hopefully, chapter 2 helped you understand enough not to fall prey to patternism any longer.

---

44. Hicks, *Women Serving*, 130, Kindle.

Huldah—a Trusted Female Prophet

The Bible also introduces us to a female prophet named Huldah. This amazing account, found in 2 Chronicles 34:19ff, happened during a time of corruption in the nation of Judah. Josiah, who became king at the age of 8 years old, was a bright spot in an otherwise dark time in the history of God's Old Testament nation. His grandfather, Manasseh, was a disaster until in later life when in a Babylonian prison he repented. Josiah's father, Amon, was a brief disaster until his own officials assassinated him. Josiah started his reign of 31 years well and ended it well, only to be followed by a son and grandson who failed to imitate his example.

The high point of Josiah's reign followed a purging of the nation from idols and the practice of idolatry. He then ordered the temple to be repaired, leading to the discovery of the Book of the Law. As Shaphan then read it to Josiah, he was smitten and realized how deeply the nation had fallen into sin through not obeying the Law. Here is what unfolded next:

2 Chronicles 34:21–22

[21] "Go and inquire of the LORD for me and for the remnant in Israel and Judah about what is written in this book that has been found. Great is the LORD's anger that is poured out on us because those who have gone before us have not kept the word of the LORD; they have not acted in accordance with all that is written in this book." [22] Hilkiah and those the king had sent with him went to speak to the prophet Huldah, who was the wife of Shallum son of Tokhath, the son of Hasrah, keeper of the wardrobe. She lived in Jerusalem, in the New Quarter.

Huldah proceeded to receive word from the Lord and sent the Lord's message to the king. Try as you might, you can find no resistance by any male to the role Huldah was fulfilling. She was not the only prophet available. Why did the leaders not go to Jeremiah instead of Huldah, for they were most certainly contemporaries? We are not told, but she was a full-fledged prophet of God in the midst of a society generally bound tightly in the clutches of patriarchy. Who can read this account and have any doubt that what occurred happened with God's absolute approval?

Queen Esther

As we next consider Queen Esther, I can't improve on what John Mark Hicks wrote, so I will just quote his astute observations.

> While there were other queens in the history of Israel, Esther stands out because a whole book tells her courageous story as the queen of Persia. It explains the origins of the Feast of Purim. That feast is an addition to the Torah. Esther authorized it. Esther added to the Torah. Esther "gave full written authority" to inaugurate the feast and provided its regulations (Esther 9:29–31). In Hebrew, "gave" is both singular and feminine. Though Mordecai was associated with the action, Esther was responsible. "The command of Esther," the Bible says, "fixed these practices of Purim" (Esther 9:32). *Esther exercised both political and religious authority over Israel.*[45]

Esther was obviously a leader from God.

Jesus, the Tradition Breaker

No one can doubt that Jesus often derailed highly valued traditions of the Jewish people. The Jewish ruler who said that Jesus could have done his miracles on the other six days of the week rather than the Sabbath spoke the truth. Yet, as you read the various accounts of his miracles and healings, it seems as though he deliberately saved many such events for sabbath days. He was forcing the issue, trying to help people see that he had to be the Messiah. Who else could do the things he did? But for those determined to disbelieve, his wonderful works were attributed to Satan himself.

---

45. Hicks, *Women Serving*, 137–8, Kindle.

It is difficult to grasp how much of a tradition breaker Jesus was in his relationships with women. We naturally tend to read through the lenses of our own societal setting, and when we do, we simply miss how shocking Jesus' relationships with women were. In this area, he was not a bit less unconventional and untraditional than in his sabbath violations (as his enemies judged it). Here are but a few of many examples of Jesus breaking traditions in this regard.

1. He openly talked with women in spite of the fact that men and women did not normally converse in public settings. It was frowned upon.

2. He took the side of a guilty woman, one caught in the very act of adultery, and thereby saved her very life. What must she have felt to hear these words: "Then neither do I condemn you," Jesus declared. "Go now and leave your life of sin" (John 8:11).

3. As mentioned earlier, five women are mentioned in the lineage of the Messiah: Tamar, Rahab, Ruth, Bathsheba, and Mary. And quite fittingly for a tradition breaker, three of them were of questionable moral background and two of them were of foreign descent, making it rather obvious that Jesus in the flesh was no pure-blooded Jew.

4. Women were in the group following Jesus and support-ed him from their own financial means—both far more countercultural than we moderns imagine.

5. Women were taught by Jesus as he also taught men—un-heard of and shocking in that societal setting.

6. The Samaritan woman at the well was the first to be told outside the circle of the apostles that Jesus was the Messi-ah and thus the first to share that good news (to evange-lize, in other words).

7. Mary of Bethany anointed Jesus, and after even his own apostles condemned her actions, he declared that her story would be told as a part of the gospel. Mark 14:9 states: "Truly I tell you, wherever the gospel is preached throughout the world, what she has done will also be told, in memory of her." This is one of few stories found in all four Gospel accounts. Any attempt to devalue a woman in the presence of Jesus never came to a good conclusion for those who attempted it. Never.

8. Women remained at the cross until Jesus was dead, but other than John, the apostles were not mentioned at all.

9. Women first saw the resurrected Jesus and first were sent by him to report it to the apostles—another example of being the first to evangelize with good news. If an evangelist is one who evangelizes, here we have the first evangelists (though not officially appointed as such).

Do you really think that such a consistent emphasis on women, often in countercultural fashion, was simply coincidental? It should be clear that if Jesus didn't value women more than men, he certainly didn't value them less. He was not simply swatting at the concepts of patriarchy; he was using a sledgehammer on it through all of these examples. He was paving the way for his final covenant with us earthlings to reach its apex prior to Judgment Day. Are we listening and watching, or are we still doggedly determined to hold on to a patriarchy that he rejected repeatedly? Will we continue to dismiss or water down Joel 2 and Acts 2? Will we allow what God said he would use to usher in via the new covenant—our daughters will prophesy, and our women be immersed in the Spirit and prophesy (Acts 2:17–18)? Will we in essence resist God himself? Or should I say, will we continue to resist God himself?

Paul, A Liberator of Women

Paul was so deeply entrenched in Jewish traditionalism, which included patriarchy as a firm foundation, that his conversion en route to Damascus was only one of the miracles that invaded his life. His views about so many things had to be radically altered that trying to imagine this is an uphill climb for modern minds. I wrote a book entitled, *The Apostle Paul: Master Imitator of Christ*.[46] His imitation of Jesus was like no other, and that included his rejection of the principles of patriarchy and the acceptance of woman as fully equal to men. The necessary changes in his views were so numerous and deeply entrenched in who he was as a person that those changes are nothing short of miraculous.

His meeting of and conversion of Lydia in Philippi was beautiful to behold. Some men are threatened by strong, dominant women, but Paul was one who both recognized spiritual gifts and encouraged them. When he later wrote about those gifts in passages like Romans 12:6–8, any mention of gender is nowhere to be found. We may well assume that women had gifts like serving and encouraging, while men had gifts like teaching and leading, but it is an assumption that would have no doubt have surprised Paul (and the Holy Spirit who inspired him to write). After Lydia and her household were converted, she tried to persuade him to come and stay at her house, and he was willing to be persuaded (Acts 16:15). Paul was indeed a master imitator of Christ, and nowhere is this more evident than in his relationships with women.

Phoebe—More Than Meets the Eye?

Romans 16:1–2 (NASB)
[1] I commend to you our sister Phoebe, who is a servant of the church which is at Cenchrea; [2] that you receive her in the Lord in a manner worthy of the saints, and that you help her in whatever matter she may have need of

---

46. Gordon Ferguson, *The Apostle Paul: Master Imitator of Christ* (Spring Hill, TX: IP, 2016).

you; for she herself has also been a helper of many, and of myself as well.

Without question, Phoebe has received a fair amount of attention in discussions about leadership roles in the church. Specifically, the word translated "servant" here, *diakonos,* can be translated simply as servant or as deacon. It is in the masculine form, which was not unusual in referring to either males or females. The discussion centers on whether she was an officially appointed deacon or not. In 1 Timothy 3, after giving the qualifications for elders, Paul gives similar qualifications for deacons in verses 8–13.

Amid this section, he inserts verse 11, which reads, "Women must likewise be dignified, not malicious gossips, but temperate, faithful in all things." The word translated "women" here (*gune*) is often translated as "wives," which could mean that Paul is giving qualifications for the wives of deacons. He did not do this in the case of the wives of elders, unless this verse is meant to apply to both, which would be odd contextually. As with other words we will examine in the context naming Phoebe, the lack of certainty would allow for either interpretation, meaning that either is possible and therefore, neither can be ruled out and is thus allowable. It is a judgment call, a matter of opinion. Phoebe could certainly have been an appointed deacon in this case. Most modern scholars take that position.

Whatever may be said about this, it is clear that she was a highly valued co-worker of Paul and sent on an important mission. His description of her makes that clear. Anyone entrusted with delivering such an important document was undoubtable a person of influence. It is possible and likely that such a person would have read the letter and even explained some of its contents as needed, since they likely would have been familiar with its contents.

A Deeper Look

The term not always discussed in her description is in verse

2, the word translated "helper," from *prostatis.* The verb form, *proistemi,* means leading or to lead (found in Romans 12:8 as one of the spiritual gifts). It is used 8 times in the New Testament, translated as "rule" or "ruling" in the KJV most of the time and in the NIV as "manage" several times. Interestingly, in 1 Timothy 5:17 it is translated as "direct the affairs" of the church, speaking of elders. It can mean to assist or care for, but based on how the translators usually translated the term, it opens the door even wider for her to have been an appointed leader in the church in Cenchrea. Based on the high praise that Paul is about to direct toward a number of other women in the following context, this seems the most likely conclusion.

Prostatis is used only once in the New Testament as a noun, although outside the New Testament the word often was used for an overseer of a group. The 2011 version of the NIV translates it as benefactor, interestingly. It almost seems as though translators were avoiding identifying her as a leader. Unfortunately, and likely inaccurately, it leaves the impression that she was simply a rich woman acting as a mail carrier at her own expense. Once again, patriarchy rears its ugly head. Whatever else might be said, the high view of women held by Paul is shown by his frequent (and unusual for the time) mentions of specific women, but especially in noting their influential roles.

Another example, Nympha, is the only leader of the church in Laodicea mentioned at all (Colossians 4:15). Does that indicate that she was the primary leader there? It's not certain, but it very likely could mean that. Although house churches were the order of the day after Christianity was declared illegal around the mid-century mark, they are mentioned specifically only four times. Twice the house church leaders named were a couple, Priscilla and Aquila (Romans 16:3–5; 1 Corinthians 16:19), once a man (Philemon verse 2), and once a woman alone, in the case of Nympha.

By this point in the book, I would imagine that most would agree that we have indeed missed much that the whole Bible has to say about women and their powerful influence and leadership. We simply have overlooked much of what has been hidden in plain sight. Nympha is one in that category. Perhaps someone would say that she only provided the meeting place and an unnamed man must have been the leader. When have we ever failed to name a designated leader? I don't think Paul did it here either.

Romans 16 and Beyond—Exceptions Multiplied

As stated previously, women were not often mentioned in meaningful ways in important documents, whether in genealogies or significant letters addressed to groups, which would include epistles. But Romans 16 doesn't just contain an exception to the practice of focusing almost entirely on males, it multiplies the exceptions. Following the introduction of the impressive Phoebe, note what follows. Also, keep in mind that Paul had not yet visited Rome in person, and the mention of names of those he already knew or knew of was his way of establishing connection with the church. Outside of God's family setting, such a practice would undoubtedly have focused on males, but this is God's family where mutuality was a sacred concept (and still is).

Paul identified many people by name in his thirteen epistles. If I counted correctly, 79 were mentioned specifically in a variety of contexts. Most of them, male and female, were Paul's fellow workers, to use a term he favored. Many of these were mentioned as either sending their greetings to others or receiving them from others, or both. Five of the men were named five or more times, with Timothy topping the list at 18. Priscilla was mentioned three times by Paul and four times by Luke in Acts, five of the seven times before her husband, Aquila.

Some have attributed this most unusual sequence to her holding a higher standing, but Paul was decidedly not influenced by social standing (1 Corinthians 1:26–30). Most believe that she was the most dominant personality of the two, and likely the most accomplished theologically. If you can accept that the spiritual gifts in Romans 12 of prophecy (there were female prophets, remember), teaching and leading, that possibility is not at all strange.

Of the scores of names found in Paul's writing, six were on the "naughty" list as those who deserted Paul, taught false doctrines, or evidently were recipients of church discipline, the type mentioned by Paul in Romans 16:17–18. The most striking use of names was a long list of Paul's co-workers in this same chapter, the final chapter of Romans. In it, 37 individuals were named or indicated, ten of which were women, eight by name (if Phoebe is included), one designated as a sister, and another as a mother. In the remainder of Paul's letters, six other women were mentioned, two of whom we will discuss.

Beginning in the greeting list of verses 3 and following, nine of the 26 individuals are women. Of these, Prisca is described as Paul's fellow worker, Junia is praised as a fellow prisoner with Paul and as an apostle, and four others are praised for their labor for the Lord (Mary, Tryphena, Tryphosa, and Persis). Only three men are complimented in these same terms (Aquila, Urbanus, and Andronicus). Read the chapter carefully and ask yourself not only why so many women were named, but the reason for such glowing descriptions given them. No answer makes logical sense other than that they were female leaders in the church at Rome.

A Female Apostle?

Verse 7 deserves special note. "Greet Andronicus and Junia, my fellow Jews who have been in prison with me. They are outstanding among the apostles, and they were in Christ before I was." The original NIV translation has Junia as Junias. History informs us that up until the thirteenth century, this person was described as a woman apostle, thus Junia. From the thirteenth century until the twentieth century, this person was depicted as a male, Junias. The power of patriarchy is at times simply astounding. Early church writers had no problem with a female apostle. But the male scholars of a later day, and all Bible translations during those centuries, succeeded in performing the first known sex change as they made Junia into a man, no doubt against her will! Happily, that unwelcome change could be, and should be, reversed. Perhaps you are wondering why the change should be reversed. This quote (from a complementarian, by the way) gives the reason.

> Apart from preconceptions about gender roles, what evidence can be adduced one way or the other on this issue? The deciding factor seems to be the existence or nonexistence of these two names in contemporary Roman inscriptions. The facts are that the feminine name Junia has been found about 250 times in such inscriptions, while the masculine form Junias has thus far been found nowhere (Lampe, "Romans 16," 223, 226). The reasonable conclusion, then, is that Junia was a woman, and that Andronicus and Junia were husband and wife.[47]

The praise offered Andronicus and Junia in this verse is high praise indeed. Fellow Jews with Paul, imprisoned with him, outstanding among the apostles, and preceding him in Christ. The word "apostle" simply means a messenger, or one sent on a mission. The term is applied in a special way to the twelve, and later in the same way to Matthias and Paul. The word "disciple" is also used in a special way of the twelve, but like the term apostle, applied more generally also. Acts 14:14 depicts Barnabas as an apostle. Galatians 1:19 calls James, the brother of Jesus, an apostle. The two mentioned here in Romans 16 were designated as apostles, a term we would likely replace with the term missionary. The point is that Paul is praising women as highly as the men, which is as countercultural as anything Jesus ever did. Paul was indeed the master imitator of his Lord.

Are Men Clueless?

Most Christian women do not want to disparage men in any

---

47. "The College Press NIV Commentary, Romans" Vol 2, online version.

way, but rather want to lift them up. Our culture tends to make men look like buffoons in an overreaction to being caught in the trap of our historical patriarchal culture. The effects of this culture in overly conservative church settings often manifests itself as if on steroids, and not only in limiting women in their God-given gifts. Christian men feel the pressure that patriarchy has put on them to lead and to portray a certain "manly" demeanor, without which they may be viewed negatively by their alpha-type male leaders.

We moderns, especially in the Western world, have little idea of how unusual the inclusion of women was in such lists or in any type of formal letter such as the epistles. The devaluation of women throughout most of history would be difficult for us to grasp without help.

In fact, if we ran the calendar back a mere century, even in America, we would be shocked. In the public sphere, women were kept in the background, seen but not heard, limited almost exclusively to the spheres of wife and mother. The fight to gain the right to vote was a bitter battle, finally resulting in the enactment of the Nineteenth Amendment in 1920, giving women the right to vote— White women, that is. Black women did not gain that same right until 1965, with the passage of the Voting Rights Act. Even after that, they were purposely hindered by discriminatory red tape, to put it mildly.

Why is all of this information important? To help us see just how countercultural much of the Bible was in describing what women did in a culture otherwise immersed in the power of patriarchy. And, as has already been shown, this was not limited to the New Testament. Far from it. Scot McKnight, a highly respected theologian and prolific author, tells of using the popular acronym, WWJD, as a segue into another similar one—WDWD (what did women do in the Bible?). In discussions with those with their theology still governed by patriarchy, he asks a good question.

In my conversations with friends after we have discussed both the

WDWD passages and the "Women Keep Silence Passages" (WKSP), I always conclude with this question: Do you permit women to do in your churches what women did in the Bible and in the early churches?[48]

He further discusses our tendency to quickly, almost primarily, gravitate to the so-called "prohibition texts" regarding woman. Using his typical cut-to-the-chase analytical expertise, he states what should not be left out of our overall approach to the subject.

Some of my friends are for and some are against women in leadership ministries. Both kinds of friends gravitate to these texts. For me, gravitating to these passages for this discussion is like asking about marriage in the Bible and gravitating toward the divorce texts. Talking marriage through the divorce texts is beyond short-sighted, if not distorting. The same applies to women in ministry texts.[49]

Injustices of Both Sexism and Racism

Again, I am just saddened by what I fully believe is in the realm of gross injustice toward women and toward people of color. That is why in my later years, I have felt compelled to address both of these injustices. Unless our attention is brought to these areas, White men (and White women to a lesser degree) will remain oblivious to what those unlike them face and feel. The degree of our lack of awareness is often simply shocking.

Early in 2023, I attended a teacher's conference in Oklahoma City. During a panel discussion, one of the teachers, a long-term resident of Oklahoma, made a statement that boggled my mind. He said that that the Oklahoma educational system had only within the last few years made it mandatory to teach the account of the Tulsa Race Riot of 1921, also called the Tulsa Race Massacre. Incredible! How does such happen, that atrocities against Black people are left out of history books and their genuine accomplishments

---

48. McKnight, *The Blue Parakeet*, 215.
49. McKnight, *The Blue Parakeet*, 213–214.

also omitted? Easy answer: White people write history books, and a majority White population doesn't notice the omissions.

The same principle operates in a culture dominated by males, particularly a religious culture. But we males, and many females within that culture simply don't notice it. Culture has all but blinded us toward the topic of women in the Bible. One of the most influential complementarians to be found, John Piper, wrote a book in 2018 entitled, *21 Servants of Sovereign Joy: Faithful, Flawed, and Fruitful*. He described the lives of spiritual giants in the history of the church, all of which were White men—no women and no persons of color. And this in a tome of 816 pages. Again, simply incredible! In 2022, he updated it to *27 Servants of Sovereign Joy: Faithful, Flawed, and Fruitful*, expanded to 1024 pages. Still no women and no persons of color. Are you really surprised?

Along with Wayne Grudem, Piper is one of the two most recognized champions of complementarianism. If you are comfortable in a spiritual world dominated by white males, that's your choice. I am extremely uncomfortable in such a world, although it has been my world for the better part of my life. But no longer. I don't think the Bible allows it. I don't think God allows it with approval. I'm with McKnight and his WDWD. Throughout the entire Bible, women did amazing things. God did not leave them and their amazing stories out of his history book. Will we study them, admire them, respect them, cherish them, or will we go straight to the so-called limitations that are found in a cultural context that has little or nothing to do with our cultural setting? It's your choice; I've made mine. I believe God has very clearly and unmistakably made his.

A Final Test

Are you ready for a final exam to show where your heart and mind are landing on this topic of women in the home and in the church? Here is a slightly altered passage from Paul. Please read it, and we will discuss your first reactions and possible conclusions.

I plead with Erastus and I plead with Stephanas to be of the same mind in the Lord. Yes, and I ask you, my true companion, help these men since they have contended at my side in the cause of the gospel, along with Clement and the rest of my co-workers, whose names are in the book of life.

What was your first thought about what the underlying issue was with Erastus and Stephanas? Was it simply a personality conflict over an off topic or was it a theological conflict of some sort, serious enough to hurt the unity of the church? Were these two men likely leaders of influence or just average members who were being a distraction to the other members? What initially comes into your mind when considering these questions? Now let's omit the slight alteration of the passage and read it as Paul wrote it.

Philippians 4:2–3
[2] I plead with Euodia and I plead with Syntyche to be of the same mind in the Lord. [3] Yes, and I ask you, my true companion, help these women since they have contended at my side in the cause of the gospel, along with Clement and the rest of my co-workers, whose names are in the book of life.

Now ask yourself the very same questions posed in the preceding paragraph. Are your answers any different? These women have contended at Paul's side, not in any way beneath him, or "under" him, and they have done it on an equal basis with the other scores of Paul's co-workers. I suspect you saw Erastus and Stephanas as leaders within the church at Philippi having considerable influence, and the issue as one of theological importance. Did you see these two women the same way? Or might you have seen their issue more as a personal disagreement that led to hurt feelings? After all, women have often been viewed as overly emotional, and thus not so inclined to be able to deal well with theological issues, right? In fact, only in the last fifty years have our Restoration Movement theological schools even allowed women to study theology.

Well, how did you do on our little exam? All of us have some unrecognized biases in multiple areas. We all read the Bible with preconceived ideas, whether we recognize it or not. Striving to eliminate as many systemic biases as possible is a noble task and one that never will end. Disciples are learners, not simply of "new" truths, but more importantly, of our unintentional, unrecognized untruths. God said that Satan was untruth personified. We must, like God, hate error in our love of truth. Error comes in many forms, and we must cultivate a deep desire to recognize it in both our thinking and actions, including the motivations behind them. God sees it all, for he knows us perfectly.

Let's not just allow him to change our thinking in any area where it is wrong; let's beg him. Thus I end this chapter begging you to at least consider all I have written on a controversial topic. Our views and practices of spiritual leadership begin with a recognition of patriarchy's motivation toward power and control. To really eliminate all the errors of leadership, what better place to begin than at the beginning. If we start there and read the entire Bible with both Satan's plan and God's plan well in mind, we will land in the right places with the right relationships. May God get us to this wonderful destination!

Chapter 8

A Missing Key in Spiritual Formation

Human beings hold such a unique place in God's scheme that we should be staggered by the very thought. We microscopic specks in comparison to the vast universe, all of it God's magnificent creation, fit into his divine plan as those chosen specially to reflect his image. Staggering indeed is the realization. Yet we live in a world described by John in these sobering words. "We know that we are children of God, and that the whole world is under the control of the evil one" (1 John 5:19). Our transformation into the image of Christ is our highest goal, our most lofty challenge amid a fallen world. We desperately need every type of help available, all of which is provided by God. But what are all those sources of divinely available help to keep us growing? We need them all; therefore we cannot afford to miss any.

This thought may come as a surprise to you, but this whole realm of male/female interrelationships remains one of those sources most often missed, or at best, significantly diluted. As our world is rapidly degenerating into the pits of hell, we must use everything at our disposal to keep growing and keep reflecting our Maker and Redeemer. The concept of spiritual growth has been sharpened in definition in recent years by using the term "spiritual formation." The very term suggests an available path, that if followed carefully and sincerely, can lead us more deeply into God's image and thus into our very purpose for living. Biblical interpretation plays a fundamental role, making misinterpretations of the most important issues a huge hindrance to needed growth. The topic of this book is one of those most important issues.

I share Jeanie Shaw's definition of spiritual formation from her recent book, *Re-Examining Our Lenses.*

> The profound relationship between interpretation and spiritual formation must be recognized and explored. Spiritual formation often implies the practice of spiritual disciplines, but it involves much more. My nuanced version defines it as "beholding God, as revealed through the incarnate Christ, with increasing clarity and giving Him the space to, through His indwelling Spirit, transform us more closely into His image, thus reflecting Him in our daily lives and relationships.[50]

God is not calling us to plod through life with just enough righteousness in us through Christ's sacrifice to avoid hell and squeeze into heaven. Living with one foot in the world and one foot in the kingdom of heaven is unacceptable to him and not even possible. The top priority in our hearts will end up controlling our lives. God is calling us into life on the mountaintops with him and his family. As overwhelming as that lofty challenge may be to contemplate, it produces in me a conviction that I don't want to miss anything that might help me ascend that mountain.

Essential Relationships in Spiritual Formation

Many types of relationships are essential to optimum spiritual formation, starting with the foundation of our personal relationship to God. Healthy family relationships supply the ideal next building block after our relationship with God. Then, we have spiritual family relationships in God's family, and these come in many forms. Parents long to have their children raised within a village of spiritual relationships of all types, from the children's friends to the older crowd who serve as surrogate moms and dads, aunts and uncles, grandfathers and grandmothers. We especially need

---

50. Shaw, *Re-Examining*, 7-8.

this broadened spiritual family in our modern world of nuclear families where such relationships within physical families are often missing, or at the least not living in close proximity.

We then consider what are often called discipling relationships with a purposeful design to call each other higher, male to male and female to female. Since I became acquainted with this concept decades ago, I have called it the *missing ingredient* in most churches. Discipling was the main concept that attracted me into the family of churches I have been a part of for nearly four decades. I've written two books on the topic and taught about "one another" Christianity since that now distant time. Sadly, this practice has too often gone missing within our own fellowship for many members and significantly minimized for the rest, with a few exceptions here and there. We need companions along the way that help us see God at work.

But what we are missing almost entirely are those kinds of spiritual relationships between brothers and sisters in Christ that prompted Paul to write Romans 16 as he did. If God is neither male nor female but possesses the finest qualities of both, both males and females must have relationships with the opposite gender that promote such learning—learning by imitating and by receiving input. To imitate someone, you first must know them well enough to understand them as individuals. To receive input, you must first build safe, healthy relationships that enable you to be open to their input.

Important Parts, Yet Incomplete

I do realize that as children, we grow up learning a lot from our parent of the opposite sex, if we are fortunate enough to have them in the home. Most have their mothers there, but far fewer have their dads in their homes. This means that more male children are going to learn the female perspective than female children are going to learn the male perspective. In either case, we all spend most of our lives as adults out of the home and thus must have ways to develop relationships with the opposite gender as a part of our ongoing spiritual formation. Also, most of our years in the home were prior to our becoming Christians, and prior to our brains maturing to the point of connecting all the dots. (Just ask rental car companies about that factor and what age 25 means to them.) This is based on a biological fact, proven beyond doubt. The home environment provides much to overall emotional formation, and if we are fortunate, also to our spiritual formation. But the rest of our years outside of the home must provide the largest portion of what we need.

Within the church setting, we are exposed to the differences in male and female perspectives through fellowship times before and after assemblies or classes, limited though they are. If we belong to a church with functioning small groups, we have more and better exposure to those of the opposite gender, but most of us aren't thinking about learning from the opposite gender in any purposeful way. In almost all church related settings, men tend to congregate with other men and women with women. When men and women do talk in those settings with each other, the content is most often about non-spiritual, ordinary matters of life rather than spiritually oriented ones. I will share more about why I believe this is the case, but my point is that we are missing or seriously diluting what I think we all need and what Jesus and Paul modeled.

A Great Starting Place

One of my early forays into developing deep relationships with women came through the door of my becoming a sort of surrogate spiritual father to both young men and young women. I remember well a time following a ministry staff meeting when one of our young male interns told me that he felt close to me and asked if he could call me dad. I pushed back quickly against the request, saying that at age 42, I was far too young to be his father. When I told my good friend, Ron Brumley, one of the elders in the church and a school principal, about it, he said that being a spiritual parent to younger people was one of our greatest roles we could provide, a true honor. He went on to explain that many of our younger disciples either didn't have a father or didn't have a good one. His point was not lost on me, and I quickly progressed to value the role of "dad" above all other roles in which I ever served.

Decades ago, my two biological children gave me a ring with the word "Dad" displayed prominently on the front. They explained that they knew I wasn't just their dad, but a father figure to many younger men and women in the church. At times, they asked me to be a dad to one of their friends who needed a dad. One of the most providential moments in my life involved meeting a young woman of college age whose relationship with me became the stuff of fairy tales. You can read about it on my website (gordonferguson.org) under the title, "Another Kind of Adoption."[51] If this article doesn't bring tears to your eyes, you may need some spiritual help getting in touch with your God-given emotions! Through the years, I have been blessed with many "adopted" sons and daughters, more of the latter than the former, not surprisingly. In my experience, women are often more finely turned to emotional relationships in general.

Not Just Incomplete, But Often Missing

We need more relationships with the opposite gender beyond those of a parent figure. I have friends who happen to be women who are nearer my own age, and I treasure my relationships with them. As I was thinking about these types of relationships several years ago, it dawned on me that I hadn't made the most of these relationships. Theresa and I often get together with couples who are close to us. During those times we talk some as couples, and I usually end up talking mostly to the brother while Theresa talks mostly to the sister. One day I realized that many of these sisters are as close to me emotionally as are their husbands. I didn't just love the guys; I loved their wives equally.

---

51. Gordon Ferguson, "Another Kind of Adoption," Gordon Ferguson Teaching Ministry, https://gordonferguson.org/gordon-ferguson14/.

The next time we were with some of these close couples, like Wyndham and Jeanie Shaw and Tom and Sheila Jones, I explained that very point to them and their husbands. I love these women and many others like them. I wanted them to know that my relationship wasn't just with their mate; quite the contrary. I love talking to my female friends. They have helped me deal with my chauvinism and unconscious sexism, along with so many other spiritual issues. Some of the best discipling I have ever received came from women. My ability to gain the most in my spiritual formation depended on them.

Speaking of the Shaws, my true brother/sister relationship with Jeanie Shaw has helped me immensely on the topic of this book. She and I have enjoyed many serious talks through the years as absolute equals. She is not one of my "women friends," but a friend who happens to be a woman. Similarly, I don't have "Black friends," but rather friends who happen to be Black. Do you see the difference? It's an important one. There is hardly anything Jeanie doesn't know about me and little that I don't know about her. Theresa and I were discipling partners with Wyndham and her for years, and as a result we know quite a lot about all areas of each other's lives through the discipling process. It is the stuff out of which genuine spiritual relationships come.

Now that our beloved Wyndham has graduated to Glory, her relationship with me is even more important. I am her big brother, her confidant and advisor, and the relationship is an equal blessing to me in multiple ways. Our present discussions, occasionally in person but most often on the phone or through email, about the women's role topic and many other topics involve a level of communication that the average disciple simply doesn't have with those of the opposite gender. When that is the case, the relationships remain shallow between brothers and sisters in most (not all) cases. More importantly, it also means that something in our spiritual formation is sadly absent.

How Are Females Viewed and Valued in the Church?

I have often said that one of the most foundational concepts for each of us in our walk with God stems from correctly viewing him and correctly understanding how he views us, for this will directly impact how we see ourselves and the two of us together in relationship. Loving him with our whole being is the greatest command in the Law. But the second greatest command is to love our neighbors as ourselves. Our closest neighbors are the spiritual ones in the family of God. Thus, a second foundational concept for each of us in our spiritual walk with those neighbors is in how we see them, how we think they see us, and how we view our relationship with them.

Women can grasp that God loves them and sees them as his precious daughters, but their view of themselves will still be significantly impacted by how they think others view them, especially males. Those views, and the feelings produced in them, begin at birth. The male figures in a female child's life can set them up to love themselves, doubt themselves, or even hate themselves. In our world of patriarchy existing from near the beginning of time, males have been given far more influence than they deserve. History says that this is true; history shouts it out, in fact. Males are perceived, consciously or unconsciously, as representatives of God in a child's life. Most children will end up seeing God in much the same way they see their earthly fathers or other significant males in their lives, for good or ill. If you are a male, do you feel the burden that I am feeling right now as I write this? Women are going to be influenced greatly by how we men have viewed and treated them from childhood to old age. It cannot be otherwise in a world like ours.

Are Women Inferior to Men?

The question just hanging in the air is this one: Are women inferior to men? Or do they more dimly reflect God's image? Dr.

Sarah Sumner, in her book, Men and Women in the Church,[52] went to great lengths to show that historically women have been viewed as inferior to men. Furthermore, because this has been the prevailing opinion for centuries, many women still view themselves as inferior to males, as if they are one step removed from God's image. Sumner introduces a significant amount of anecdotal evidence to support her view that this is common in evangelical circles among both men and women today. Since I view women as equals, often superior intellectually and spiritually, I was shocked at the true stories she shared. I was also shocked at the quotes from well-known early church writers like Augustine and Tertullian who stated this supposed inferiority in bold and unmistakable terms. Shocking, I'm saying! Such quotes today would not simply be viewed as politically incorrect but would light up the internet to the point of overloading cyberspace.

I agree with the logic involved in what egalitarians are saying. If women can lead in any other field, effectively I might add, and yet are quite limited in church leadership, the question about them being somehow inferior is logically raised. The complementarians define masculinity and femininity mostly in terms of family roles and how those roles interrelate by gender. It is obvious that they believe that Eve as a "helpmeet" was created primarily to serve Adam and to bear and raise his children. In the "Complementarian Bible," *Recovering Biblical Manhood and Womanhood: A Response to Evangelical Feminism,* the authors deliver a foundational quote in the first chapter (in their own applied capital letters, thus showing these assertions to be fundamental to their overall position):

AT THE HEART OF MATURE MASCULINITY IS A SENSE OF BENEVOLENT RESPONSIBILITY TO LEAD, PROVIDE FOR AND PROTECT WOMEN IN WAYS APPROPRIATE TO A MAN'S DIFFERING RELATIONSHIPS.

---

52. Sarah Sumner, *Men and Women in the Church: Building Consensus on Christian Leadership* (Westmont, IL, IVP, 2003).

AT THE HEART OF MATURE FEMININITY IS A FREEING DISPOSI-
TION TO AFFIRM, RECEIVE AND NURTURE STRENGTH AND LEADER-
SHIP FROM WORTHY MEN IN WAYS APPROPRIATE TO A WOMAN'S
DIFFERING RELATIONSHIPS.[53]

Should it not strike us as strange that quotes like the above focus on the term *lead* when it doesn't even appear in the passage? A basic problem that egalitarians have with complementarians is that women are defined almost exclusively in relation to their roles with men, not as separate human beings in their own right with their individual gift sets that may have little or nothing to do with being wives and mothers. Besides defining what it is to be female, mainly in terms of a woman's relationship to a husband, females also have often been defined as having the primary purpose of bearing and raising children.

While that is a primary purpose (not "the" primary purpose), this view can further downplay females as individual persons made in the image of God with all the gifted creativity that goes with this image. For centuries, any type of leadership roles for women were limited not simply based on biblical interpretation, but also on the basis of the assumed inferiority of women. Do you see that the latter would have to influence the former? Now, almost no one outwardly subscribes to the concept of female inequality, but in the minds of egalitarians, it is subtlety taught and everywhere implied. I agree with that assessment.

Spiritual Beings and Sexual Beings—the Challenges

I am not underestimating the importance of taking seriously the potential dangers of temptations in the sexual realm, even between spiritual brothers and sisters in Christ. Dr. Sumner's book addressed this topic quite directly. She was open and vulnerable about both her husband's and her own sexual temptations. She

---

53. Grudem, *Recovering*, 35–36.

broadened her discussion beyond temporary lust issues to include things such as immodest dress by women and pornography viewing and addiction. I was pleasantly surprised that a well-known, highly educated person like her would be so vulnerable and honest about a topic that is almost taboo in many religious circles. Kudos to her for her convictions and courage! As she has done in other places in her book, she argues that none of us can live righteous lives consistently without what I usually term *discipling*—having other people in your life. If you know me, you know I am shouting "AMEN" to her comment right now! One of my favorite definitions of discipling is that it is God's way of helping us deal with sin at the temptation level before it can enter our lives and devastate us. It is more than that, but this is a vital part of the definition.

I was moved by reading the chapter in Sumner's book, but found myself wondering why that chapter was in a theological book. Of course, practical applications are always good in any book or oral lesson, but I was left feeling unsettled for some reason. Gradually, some thoughts started connecting the dots that the book didn't clearly connect. There is something about our views of women and the challenge of sexual purity that is far more connected that we have likely understood. It finally dawned on me that this connection is directly tied to what has hindered or blocked genuine personal relationships between brothers and sisters in the church. The only thing that can remove the block is seeing women as God sees them and relating to them according to his plan, in genuine family relationships.

An Inescapable Assumption?

The common view of complementarian oriented thinkers effectively limits or prohibits entirely meaningful relationships between men and women disciples. This view, perhaps unknowingly and unintentionally, is produced by their primary definition of women as wives and mothers. To define women in this way makes it logical to view them mostly in their reproductive capacity, thus in their sexual composition. That alone can lead to the worldly view by the masculine crowd that women exist primarily as sexual beings. Those outside of Christ, particularly males, are guilty as charged by Peter when he spoke of those "with eyes full of adultery, they never stop sinning" (2 Peter 2:14). Our world is sex-crazed and so far from biblical standards in areas of morality that it is difficult to believe how fast and far the degradation has come.

As followers of Jesus, maintaining sexual purity in our male minds (the view I am addressing, as a man) which are influenced strongly by our eyesight, is a spiritual matter and a male responsibility. That spiritual mindset includes how we view females as whole persons. If we focus on their physical beauty and their unique physical attributes, sexual purity is going to be a much bigger challenge. If we focus on them as persons made in the image of God, with their intellects and spirituality, their spiritual dreams and struggles, the challenge is going to be reduced substantially. Any human function in this brief life doesn't begin to compare with what our true God-given nature involves, namely the spiritual capacity to spend eternity with God. Why then do we place so much emphasis on matters of a temporal nature when defining women? Something is missing in our whole approach to this definition. Make no mistake about it, the prevailing cultural emphasis on the physical composition of women complicates and diminishes the possibility of males relating to women as Jesus and Paul did. That fact is the essence of why I included this chapter in the book. Spiritual brother/sister relationships are designed by God to be an integral part of our spiritual formation. Worldly views, whether we see them in ourselves or not, produce major roadblocks to what should be a wonderful blessing in spiritual maturation.

While childbirth is an important and valued role, surely God had so much more in mind when he created women. If not, women who aren't mothers have little value. And what are women to be once they become empty nesters (which for some women occurs while they are still in their 30s)? In our nuclear families, the role of grandparents is also quite different than in previous times. Centuries of patriarchal thinking and practice has also hindered men's spirituality because it tends to bring attitudes of entitlement toward women rather than those attitudes describing Jesus in Philippians 2, viewing all others above ourselves and their needs above our own. This illustrates the very important need for retraining Christian men in how to holistically and spiritually view women. Are they to be seen primarily as home-based creatures who are by definition subservient to men, or are they to be seen (and treated) as absolute equals? That very point is will determine whether we view one another primarily as sexual entities by gender or persons made in the image of God, no matter the gender.

It is a Matter of Focus

If we are serious about the principle of 2 Corinthians 4:18 and focus on the "unseen," this "unseen" focuses on the eternal part of women who are made in the image of God. This places the sexual temptation into a lesser place, hopefully by a wide margin. Furthermore, I don't know how to focus on the unseen part of another person without getting to know that part of them. I think the common view of women as lesser beings has stilted the spirituality of both men and women. It paves the way to see both males and females in too much of a physical way, thus lowering the value of both. I would also argue that without males developing spiritual relationships with females beyond what we typically have done, our growth has been stilted because women have so much to teach us about spirituality through those relationships. I don't want to think that I can only gain from their spirituality if they write it in a book. Relationships are personal by definition.

But, and this is a big "but" to me, another part of the retraining is learning how to relate to sisters in the church on a personal yet spiritual basis. This is why I included details about my own process in this area, which has resulted in many blessings. I think we are missing way too much by our lack of relationship with the opposite gender. Please read the next sentence carefully.

> I believe that we have traditions in our movement about male/female relationships that are as deep (and often unrealized) as our traditions about male/female roles.

I can describe how to develop those genuine, spiritual relationships with women in much more detail, complete with describing the cautions (which I follow myself very carefully). But one of my main concerns in this chapter is aimed thus: if men viewed women as equals intellectually, emotionally, and spiritually, the temptation to entertain impure thoughts toward them would be greatly diminished—especially in the church. I think this point can be proved, and the implications of it can provide us with some wonderful opportunities that we are now likely missing. If God has all the attributes of both males and females, as a male I will remain incomplete without the spiritual influence in my life of women, and vice versa.

To limit that influence as only coming from a spouse is woefully incomplete in the grand scheme of things. Paul was single by choice and sometimes he gave such direct advice to others. Mates die. Unfortunately, divorce does occur. Where is that spiritual influence from the opposite gender going to come from then? I think the answer is obvious. Some men appear to be much more comfortable with a spiritual father/daughter relational concept than a brother/sister one. Jesus' example and his words in passages like Mark 10 show that he was comfortable with both. Romans 16 is proof positive that Paul was also. Are we? Can we be? More importantly, should we be?

The Path Toward Discarding Worldly Views

Let me say upfront that while my temptations to view women solely on the physical level can present themselves, I have very few temptations to think wrongly about sisters in Christ. I believe at the root this is a relational issue and one that this chapter address-es. Many years ago, as a ministry staff member, I changed ministry groups within our large church. In the new group was an attractive single sister, and I believe she was a very spiritual person. How-ever, due in part to her choice of clothing at times, looking in her direction was a challenge for me in keeping my mind pure. I sus-pect she was not fully aware of just how strongly men are affected by exposed skin in the leg and chest areas. I can't imagine that a spiritual woman can be aware of the degree of temptation her im-modest dress can produce in us males, and she then continues to dress in this way. So, I'll give this sister the benefit of the doubt. I will also add that prevailing views of women as primarily sexual beings is a huge part of the temptation of worldly women to dress immodestly. The advertising world is ample evidence of that fact, where beautiful women in skimpy clothing are used to promote their products, many of which have absolutely nothing to do with either women or clothing.

But back to my story. I did what we all should do with tempta-tions. I brought it into the light at the temptation level before it put down roots. I talked to the male ministry leader in my new group and was honest about the sinful attraction I had. He gave me a per-spective that proved to be true, thankfully, and thus very helpful from then on. It ties in quite directly to the main point of this chap-ter. He said that the attraction was likely based on the mystique in-volved. I didn't yet really know the sister, and he advised that once I got to know her as a spiritual sister, the temptation would likely go away. It turned out that he was entirely correct. She became like a spiritual daughter to me and has remained such. If I had it to do all over, I would have either talked to her about her sensual clothing myself or asked a women's ministry leader in the group to do it. But when I got to know the young sister as a person, the mystique disappeared and the sensual temptation along with it.

Why did I stop having that temptation with that sister? I got to know her and she me. We talked about meaningful things in our lives, not just surface things, but who we were spiritually with our God. To do that, I had to view her as a person and an equal person. It wasn't about roles in the church, but it was about who we really were as persons. Although this situation took place many years ago, I was already figuring out how to view women and their value and equality with me. I treasure women. I treasure my relationships with them. I have experienced a growing awareness of the principles which help explain the relationships both Jesus and Paul enjoyed with woman and have enabled me to enjoy those same types of relationships.

Caution is Essential

So what happens if we begin to develop a wrong kind of attraction to one of our friends of the opposite sex? Be very careful, of course. Sumner answers that very question in her book with a list of about 20 things to help ensure that we don't stray in any way with a brother or sister (or any other member of the opposite sex for that matter). As one brother summed, be pure, and be smart. For me, some of Sumner's recommendations are a bit too cautious, but they may be right on target for others. We are all different in our background experiences and in our basic make-up as humans. For those of us who are married, the nature of our sexual relationship is a factor as well. Theresa and I have enjoyed a wonderful relationship in this area, thankfully, so this likely has made me less vulnerable to temptations outside of marriage. That is the clear intent of what Paul wrote about this topic in 1 Corinthians 7:2–4. The older I've become, the less sexual temptations are a problem. As I noted previously, any sexual attraction to a sister in Christ has been a rarity for a long, long time, and much of that stems from the change in my heart in how I view women.

I love my sisters and my relationships with them. I try to be very sensitive regarding where their comfort zone is with me. One thing I believe for sure, and that is that our comfort zones with brothers and sisters will be largely determined by the degree of equality with which we view one another. The truth makes us free, and the truth about what and who a woman really is will free us up to relate in ways that the world knows little about. I can enjoy the attractiveness of all people equally without so much as a hint of anything sexual involved. Jesus surely was able to do the same, and we are to become more like him, right?

Always a Matter of Life and Doctrine

This subject of men and women relationships in the church is far more important than simply getting our doctrine right. It is about getting our relationships right. And since relationships are the most important thing in God's world, you can safely assume that his doctrines are going to aid those relationships, not hinder them. That one assumption may well play a more vital role in our approach to biblical interpretation than we might now imagine. If we get this wrong, women are robbed of their rightful place in the family of God, robbed of relationships with their brothers in Christ, and relegated to the outer court as they were during the Greco-Roman culture of the first century and well as through many other periods of history and some contemporary settings. How sad! Men, even the ones doing the robbing, rob themselves of the opportunities to learn from the women's perspectives, which can often be more spiritual than theirs. They rob themselves of the opportunity to experience deeper spiritual formation with God working through their sisters in Christ to provide it. In the world of patriarchy, the foundation of complementarianism, there are no winners, male or female. Only losers. Sadness is multiplied, as "what might have been" is lost, and unless we change, lost forever.

By this point in the book, we have viewed women from many different vantage points in our efforts to see them as God sees them. When we see the circle of female friends Jesus had, this becomes enormously helpful, if we will open our eyes and allow it to be. Paul's circle of female friends amply demonstrates that the example of Jesus was not to be considered unique, but rather imitated. And as the title of my book on Paul suggests, he was indeed the master imitator of Christ, including in this realm.

I have a question to ask, following the examination of the relationships Jesus and Paul had with women. Would any of us write anything like Paul wrote in Romans 16 about our relationships with our spiritual sisters? Have we ever? No one else in antiquity prior to Paul had. In looking at the lives of Jesus and Paul, I am left with some questions. Can brothers and sisters be friends? I mean, real friends? I think we often allow our cautions to block true friendships with those of the opposite gender, and that's not good. It may be a fine line to walk, but it can be walked if we are keeping in step with the Spirit. Galatians 5:16 is an important promise along these lines. "But I say, walk by the Spirit, and you will not carry out the desire of the flesh." Otherwise, the examples of Jesus and Paul must be viewed as exceptions and the wording of Mark 10:29–30 summarily dismissed. Read it.

> [29] "Truly I tell you," Jesus replied, "no one who has left home or brothers or sisters or mother or father or children or fields for me and the gospel 30 will fail to receive a hundred times as much in this present age: homes, brothers, sisters, mothers, children and fields—along with persecutions—and in the age to come eternal life.

But why have sisters in Christ if we cannot relate to them as we do our own physical sisters—at least to that extent? As I previously wrote, I believe that women are the crowning pinnacle of humankind. When I use the "saving the best for last" idea in teaching, I usually do it in a way that comes across as somewhat humorous, but even then, the sisters appreciate my high view and appreciation of them, because they sense I'm not quite just joking. I am actually serious regarding women being the height of creation. It is but one man's opinion, but it is decidedly this one man's opinion. If spirituality is the most important thing about us, I simply must hold to a very high view of women. This provides at least a part of the reason behind my willingness to restudy the whole area of the women's roles in the church and to be ready to do battle against all forms of sexism, conscious and unconscious. Sexism and racism both fall under the umbrella of oppression, and since Jesus came to free the oppressed (Luke 4:18), we as his followers have the obligation to carry on what he started and not avoid dealing with any form of oppression. He certainly didn't.

Practical Advice

Before closing this chapter, I need to add a few more practical bits of advice.

1. **Age matters.** Keep in mind that I write this book as an octogenarian. What I can be perfectly comfortable with in my relationships with sisters in Christ might not have been true at a young age. My spiritual "daughters" are a big group now at my age, and most women in the church are kids to me. The temptation factor is thus affected significantly by that age difference and by age itself. My physical desires in marriage are much decreased compared to our earlier days, and that fact alone matters a lot in my case. Age may or may not be a factor in your case, but at least give it some thought.

2. **Appearance matters.** Paul's statement in Ephesians 5:3 provides us with a good compass. "But among you there must not be even a hint of sexual immorality, or of any kind of impurity, or of greed, because these are improper for God's holy people." I occasionally have a meal or a coffee in a public place with a sister in Christ besides my wife. Usually it is with a much younger woman, and anyone who saw us would assume she was my daughter, and from a spiritual vantage point, she is. Sometimes the sister is nearer my age, and in those cases, it is most often

at a spiritual conference where other disciples are present at the same café or restaurant. Very occasionally, it may be in more of a private location, but always among a lot of people. Otherwise, I always avoid being alone with a female outside my family in private settings. I take what Paul wrote very seriously.

3. **Comfortability matters.** I am very comfortable with women and have been for most of my life. But I am very sensitive to the comfortability level of any women with whom I spend time. I ask questions in a way that casually suggests ideas or possibilities without creating any sense that I have foregone conclusions in mind. For example, since I have written a number of books, I am often asked by those in and out of the church about how one goes about the book writing process. If a sister asks, I give options regarding where we might converse about the matter. Here is a good example of how I might state those options. "We could come early or stay after church services Sunday to sit down and talk a bit. Or perhaps we could avoid interruptions by grabbing a cup of coffee and talking at a nearby coffeehouse. Or we could just talk on the phone or have a FaceTime conversation. Which would you prefer?" The comfortability discussion could be expanded into other areas, such as hugging one another in greeting, as is common in our church. I always follow the lead of the sister in this case. Some hug me like a daughter would and some hug with much less close contact. I follow their lead, since I'm comfortable with whatever they are.

4. **Honesty matters.** We have to be honest with ourselves. If a person or a situation brings a temptation to the surface, recognize and admit it. In my many years of ministry, I

have not done or said anything off-color with a woman, in or out of the church. When talking to women outside the church, I introduce my wife and God quickly into the conversation. On a few rare occasions, I have been around a woman who made me uncomfortable, who gave me something like a nervous feeling. As described earlier, if I get to know them better, the mystique disappears. But the setting in which I get to know them is always a very safe place, like in a church fellowship time. If that doesn't happen, I keep my distance both physically and emotionally. I am honest with myself, and my wife will be honest with me if she sees or senses anything that might be questionable. A few times she has felt the need to ask the question of me as to whether I was being friendly or flirtatious. Regardless of my answer, if she was uncomfortable, I was uncomfortable and made sure not to leave even a "hint" of anything that would possibly look inappropriate.

In summary, I am not even close to dismissing or diminishing the challenges of developing and maintaining spiritual relationships between brothers and sisters in Christ. We are living in a godless, immoral time in history, especially in the Western world. At the same time, I know how much my relationship with my friends who are female have enriched my life in delightful ways. In imitation of Adam and Eve as the original *imago Dei*, I strive along with my wonderful wife to be the best representatives of God possible as a married couple. In imitation of Jesus and Paul, I strive equally to do the same with my spiritual sisters. Marriages like mine stand out in this society. Few remain married for 59 years as we have; few remain faithful to their vows of a lifetime of sexual purity; and few who do manage to remain married and faithful are still as much in love as we are. God's miracle, truly.

I revel in the example we offer in our marriage. I also revel in the examples of spiritual relationships with sisters through which my life has been changed and abundantly blessed. As I said at the outset of this chapter, the concept of spiritual formation suggests a specific track which can be followed with predictably positive results in becoming increasingly more like Christ. Without relationships between males and females in God's family that are *true* family relationships, that track will always be lacking. Join me in making sure that this does not happen!

Chapter 9

Parting Thoughts

Writing about any topic and putting it into a published book means that you have hopefully studied the topic in depth and taken a significant amount of time to meditate and pray about it. As a friend once put it, you should bathe it in prayer. Amen to that! I have done that for several years before submitting my writing for publication in book form. The most emotionally challenging part for me in writing about a complex topic, especially a controversial one, is that the more you learn, the more you realize you don't yet know. You simply cannot read and digest everything on a subject. Thus, you must reach a point where you believe you understand the subject and its complexities well enough to help further the learning of those who read what you write. As always, my target audience is the average Christian, not the trained theologian. The latter type may hopefully learn something from what I write, but I am focused on those who have not studied the topic in depth yet and need a good introduction to it.

Digging Out the Roots

To understand the complexities of a subject and then state it in simpler terms, I have found one approach to be absolutely essential. Let me illustrate. After I finished writing most of this book, I read another book that really affected me emotionally, *A Church Called Tov*, by Scot McKnight and Laura Barringer. The word *tov* is the Hebrew word for good or goodness. Half the book is about leaderships which block *tov*, and half the book is about the qualities of a *tov* church. It is not a book about women or women's roles per se, but about church leadership and what churches ought to become, complete with suggestions for a path to follow to get there. The part about toxic church leadership is gut-wrenching to read. It seemed to me that two factors are at the foundation of toxic leadership: narcissistic leaders, and the lack of true team leadership that would eliminate such destructive leadership or largely limit its deadly effects. While strong, prophetic leadership is needed and biblical, to be like Jesus, it must be servant-based.

The author notes that far too many narcissistic leaders end up in church leadership, exerting the majority of power and control, even if they have an apparent team around them. They also control the so-called team, who become simply "yes men and women." A significant question was raised about whether narcissists are attracted to leadership or once in leadership, their narcissistic tendencies blossom into full bloom. McKnight answered his own question with a no doubt correct answer: both/and. Absolute power absolutely corrupts. One person, especially a male, who holds the majority of control is a train wreck waiting to happen. History could not make this point clearer.

The one most relevant observation in his book as it pertains to my book led me to a conclusion I had not thought of before. In describing what a *tov* church should look like, several spiritual qualities are described. The chapter on empathy includes a discussion of the need to show compassion and concern for different types of people, but the ways women are viewed and treated was suggested to be a sort of litmus test for the whole. Here is a good summary quote, emphasizing this point.

Though here we will focus primarily on how churches can become more empathetic toward women—because of what has happened to women in so many churches—everything we say can equally be applied to racism, classism, and other isms that degrade our fellow divine-image bearers. How the church treats women is often a barometer of its culture and how it will treat people in general.[54]

The insight that struck me after reading this conclusion, with which I completely agree, is that all errors have a starting place. All sin and the damage caused has a beginning, and to reverse the damage, that juncture where the train went off the tracks must be discovered, exposed, and correction begun. For example, as a minister with loads of experience in practical counseling, I follow this principle with those who have emotional and spiritual issues that they do not understand, issues which are blocking their spiritual formation. I believe we need to explore their past to discover the spot where their train left its tracks. I have a definite process I use to help discover this spot, but it is beyond the scope of this discussion.

Another good illustration of how root issues must be discovered before progress can be made is in the area of false biblical doctrines. In my very first book, *Prepared to Answer,* I dealt with many spiritual doctrines that I believe to be false. Each of them begins with one basic presupposition, which if granted, then provides the support to the whole philosophy. Calvinism is a classic example of this principle. The T of their TULIP system, total depravity, forms the foundation. If this is accepted, the four other tenets of the system make sense. Total depravity leads logically to unconditional election, limited atonement, irresistible grace, and perseverance of the saints. I could mention other doctrines that took a lot more work to uncover that first presupposition, but Calvinism is sufficient to make the point. As mentioned earlier, patternism is often our presupposition.

More Than Meets the Eye

By now, you may be wondering what this has to do with the women's role. It has to do with the necessity of discovering

---

54. Laura Barringer and Scot McKnight, *A Church Called Tov: Forming a Goodness Culture that Resists Abuses of Power and Promotes Healing* (Carol Stream, IL: Tyndale, 2020), 104, Kindle.

the precise spot where the error began so that we can correct it. We must see the genesis of taking the wrong road, and the basic presuppositions that led to an erroneous big picture conclusion which then supports multiple small picture conclusions. The *Tov* book didn't label it as that fateful starting place, but implied it in affirming that how we view and treat women is the best indicator of how we will view and treat others of all types. We cannot begin to fix the many ills brought on by patriarchy, which includes toxic church leadership and a whole host of other toxicities, without returning to the spot where it all started, namely Genesis 3:16. This spot began with men dominating women but quickly moved to men dominating other men as the desire for power and control ultimately dominated humanity.

While the *Tov* book helped me further crystalize the concept, I had previously stated it in a speech at the elders' retreat in 2023 as already mentioned. My assigned topic was how evangelists and elders could work together as a team. I approached the subject in much the same way I did in chapter 3 of this book, through the lens of patriarchy. Although it wasn't in my notes or PowerPoint presentation, near the end I said something to this effect: "Honestly, I don't think we can fix relational issues in our male leadership until we first fix our views of women."

What was in the back of my mind then was brought to the forefront by the quote in McKnight's and Barringer's book. The almost unbelievable evils of patriarchy's unquenchable thirst for power and control must be stopped where they first began, in the power struggle between men and women when sin first entered the world.

Ask, Seek, Knock

At this point some of you may be asking, so where do we go from here? If I have made valid points in this book about women and men, what changes do we need to make in the way we do things? What steps would it be wise to take? Is there any advice about what to do and what not do? I hope that I have left no doubt that changes need to be made in the way we handle things in the body of Christ, the Christian community.

However, it seems to me that it would be a mistake for me to try to spell out some practical plan. I do believe that I can say this: First, all of us need to rely on Jesus' teaching to ask, to seek, and to knock, believing that God will graciously provide a way forward. We should do nothing without prayer. Second, it seems to me this is where followers of Jesus need to wrestle with the principles that we have discussed, and in each location formulate their own plan of action, realizing that the exact way they seek to implement these principles may be different from the way some other congregation seeks to do that. We simply must be okay with that. This is where we need to rely on the message of Romans 14 and practice unity in diversity. Additionally, this is where we must show grace. We will make mistakes, but we can learn from them and make more changes. Surely some new mistakes that we make while sincerely seeking to please God can't be as bad as some that we've made in the past. Third, we need to keep learning from each other. We are on this journey together.

We, the disciples of Jesus, must be a light in the world. That is something we cannot be, if we simply hold to the status quo.

> *O Jesus, your kingdom come, your will be done, on earth as it is in heaven. Please take us back to Genesis 1 and Eden in your kingdom on earth now, and teach us to keep Satan's ugly hands out of it. Let your dream of mutuality between the genders and the dream of peace and unity in your new creation begin again.*
> *Amen and Amen!*

These and many more books by
Gordon Ferguson
are available at www.ipibooks.com

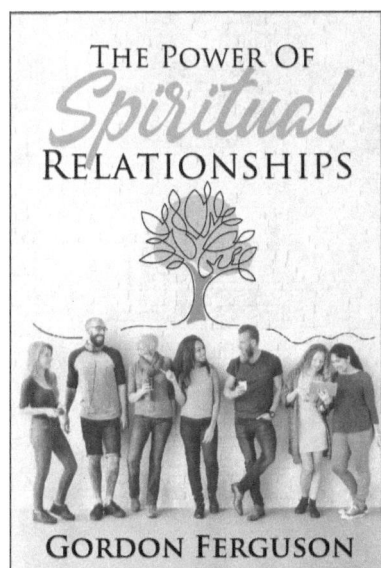

For more articles and information about Gordon go to:
www.GordonFerguson.org

www.ingramcontent.com/pod-product-compliance
Lightning Source LLC
Chambersburg PA
CBHW021636120626
46545CB00002B/568